T0368228

Finding Love
in an Upside-Down World

Finding Love in an Upside-Down World

PATRICIA E. FLINN

To order additional copies of this book, contact:
Xlibris
844-714-8691
www.Xlibris.com
Orders@Xlibris.com
861161

For

Gene, Mick, and Helen

CONTENTS

Prologue...ix

Chapter 1: The Beginning...1

Chapter 2: Relativity 12

Chapter 3: The Cosmic Dance: Flux, Motion, Change 20

Chapter 4: Aberrant Variables in Closed Systems...................26

Chapter 5: The Law of Attraction 31

Chapter 6: Parallel Universes and Multiple Realities.................37

Chapter 7: Synchronicity and the Collective Unconscious............45

Chapter 8: The Force of Gravity on Mass in Motion.................50

Chapter 9: Thoughts Become Reality.................................56

Chapter 10: When Anti-Particles Collide With Light Photons 58

Chapter 11: From Quarks to Quacks 63

Chapter 12: Radioactive Interactions across Time and Space..........67

Chapter 13: The X-Factor 74

Chapter 14: String Theory and the Law of Entanglement 80

Chapter 15: Quantum Leaps..91

Chapter 16: Frequency, Vibration, and Wave Fluctuation............101

Chapter 17: Electromagnetic High-Energy Exchanges 109

Chapter 18: The First Law of Thermodynamics.......................113

Chapter 19: Entropy 117

Chapter 20: Heisenberg's Uncertainty Principle........................119

Chapter 21: Black Holes and the Disappearance of Light............125

Chapter 22: When Fission Meets Fusion 128

Chapter 23: E=mc2 133

Chapter 24: Newton's Law: What Goes Up, Must Come Down..... 137

Chapter 25: Manifesting 142

Chapter 26: Mind and Molecular Structures 155

Chapter 27: Jumbo and the Law of Inertia 161

Chapter 28: Nature Abhors a Vacuum... 167

Chapter 29: Believing is Seeing 174

Chapter 30: Going Nuclear 183

Chapter 31: Singularity and Connection.. 191

Chapter 32: Chaos Theory on the Subatomic Level...................... 197

Chapter 33: Intention and Effect... 204

Chapter 34: The Speed of Light in an Ever Expanding Universe 208

Chapter 35: Lost in the Void... 211

Chapter 36: The Zero Point Field.. 215

Chapter 37: Orbiting the Nucleus 220

Chapter 38: And Death Shall Have No Dominion........................224

PROLOGUE

I *AM. YOU ARE. We exist.* Therefore, we all have stories to tell. This is my story. Obviously you don't have to read it. But if you do, you might enjoy a laugh here or there, or you might begin to think about your own life and how it magically and mysteriously unfolds from day to day.

Like it or not, we're here in this three dimensional world. We think everything around us is composed of solid mass and predictable matter, controlled by scientific laws like gravity, motion, cause and effect. But physicists have discovered another world inside of this one that is so strange, different, and unpredictable, it staggers the mind and imagination. Composed of atoms, particles, neutrons, photons, quarks, and the tiniest substances that defy the laws of common sense this universe is the rabbit hole come alive in Lewis Carroll's *Alice in Wonderland.*

Particles become waves depending upon who is observing them; electrons communicate with one another in ways no one can understand; things can be in two places at the same time; matter and energy are the same thing; and things can be alive and dead at the same time— Schrodinger's Cat.

As physicists probe and learn more about this fantastic quantum world the weirder it becomes. Pascual Jordan, a theoretical/ mathematical physicist published a paper claiming that *observations not only disturb what is being looked at, but they produce it.*

Werner Heisenberg, a German theoretical physicist, wrote that atoms and other elementary particles are not even real; they are just possibilities or potentialities waiting to become something once they are acted upon by invisible forces.

Max Planck argued that everything we talk about, everything we regard as existing is the result of our consciousness.

"All matter originates and exists only by virtue of a force which brings the particle of an atom to vibration and holds this most minute solar system of the atom together. We must assume behind this force the existence of a conscious and intelligent mind."

This is mind-blowing, eye-opening, heavy stuff! Thinking about it raises all kinds of questions that seem to have no clear answers. If our consciousness, feelings, and thoughts create our reality does this mean the life we are living is itself a dream, as Shakespeare once wrote?

Are fate and destiny set in stone or are they just open doors into infinite possibilities waiting to be chosen by us and entered freely and willingly?

No wonder so many of these brilliant physicists went nuts. And yet there is something quite magical and awe-inspiring about all this.

If the power of our own minds, and thoughts give us what we dream about then life really is a miracle, as Albert Einstein once said. It is a wondrous tale we write from the secrets depths of our boundless imagination that has no beginning and no end.

And since we all have tales to tell, here is mine. A wonderful love story, I once imagined and lived.

CHAPTER ONE

The Beginning

When the word was made flesh

I T'S HARD TO say when I came into existence. Theologians and mystics insist I was always here. That life has no beginning and no end. That's not entirely a religious argument either. Scientists know energy can never be destroyed. Only changed. Steam condenses into water. Water evaporates into steam and so on and so on. In that case maybe my consciousness was always here waiting to take on form to see what the experience might be like. An experiment, of sorts.

Then again, I might have begun only on the night my mother, Helen, and father, Lou—we called him Mick--, went dancing at the Transfer Station in Jersey City and then decided to take a little stroll under a moonlit sky. After a few Gin and Tonics in McDuffy's Bar, they wound up in bed at the New Yorker Hotel in Manhattan. All it took was a little bouncing around under clean crisp sheets and before they knew what hit them, they created me, a little embryo floating around in the messy murky sea of my new mother's womb.

I officially entered time, space, and the third dimension, on May 16, 1951 in St Mary's hospital on Fourth Street in Hoboken, New Jersey. A colorful neighborhood to say the least. Directly across from the hospital was Our Lady of Grace Church where a few years later I would attend Sunday mass, make my first holy communion, and become at the age of ten the Queen of the May Day procession held in honor of the blessed mother.

One block away from OLG church was Boswell's Funeral parlor where people who never made it successfully out of the hospital wound up.

I remember my many trips to Boswell's with my mother who enjoyed her visits there almost as much as people enjoy going to the movies on Saturday night. I often wondered how she came to know so many dead people, but now I believe she didn't know many of them.

It was just her way of coping when life inside the five room cold water flat where we lived became overwhelmingly boring.

Spending time in Boswell's gave her a chance to dress up, socialize, and reflect on the mystery of life. Gazing down into an open coffin and seeing rock-hard heads lying motionless forever on silky white pillows was Helen's way of acknowledging that others, like herself, were trapped in a future gone terribly awry.

For me Boswell's was an introduction to nature. Flowers of every color, shape and variety peeked out and smiled at me from tall vases, wicker baskets, and heart-shaped floral displays that surrounded the coffins and perfumed the room with the heavy sweet scent of dying roses. By the time I was five I knew lilies were white, tulips were yellow, roses were red, and daffodils were gold and grew in abundance.

Since 99 percent of Hoboken consisted of concrete sidewalks and treeless streets this knowledge was really valuable to a child learning about the world around her. Fourth and Adam Street, the locale of our cold water flat, was also educational. It was an Italian and Irish neighborhood and by the time I was seven I learned a great deal about the conflicts and rivalries that ensued when Italian and Irish families lived together in cramped tenements.

My mother was never one for hiding her true feelings and so when the Italian SanGiorgo Festival came to town in early September and set up a bandstand beneath our window, she didn't think twice about swearing and cursing at the "damn dagos" who were keeping her up, singing *Trieste Mia, Via Con Me, and Varca Lucente* until long after midnight.

When my Irish-born grandmother, Sarah, moved into the neighborhood, she cooked corn beef and cabbage on Saturday nights after her husband, Patrick, arrived home from working his job as a cop on the Hoboken police force.

Mrs. Napoli, the barber's wife, who was forever sweeping and scrubbing the street in front of her house, insisted Sarah shut her windows so that the awful stink of her Irish, overcooked cabbage wouldn't poison the entire neighborhood.

There was no love lost between the two nationalities all through the forties and fifties. It wasn't until the Cubans arrived by the boatloads in the 1960s to flee Castro's revolution that peace was finally declared and the "filthy Cubans" became the new crowd of invaders the Irish and Italians could now despise.

Despite Mrs. Napoli's opinion about Irish cooking, my grandmother, was an excellent cook. In fact, after her young husband died,-- poor Patrick was shot dead one night breaking up a brawl in a downtown saloon by some crazy man with a gun—Sarah had to work to support her five young children. She was eventually hired to cook in the local orphanage that was run by the Sisters of Charity. These nuns were my first teachers since they also ran the grammar school attached to the church.

How she managed to raise five kids—one of whom was my mother— and hold a job that demanded long hours and careful preparation is beyond me. She made breakfast, lunch, and dinner for the orphans, many of whom were the unwanted love babies of wayward women who wound up pregnant without husbands or families to support them.

The nuns in charge were not the easiest of bosses either. Their moods varied from day to day depending upon the weather, what they ate for dinner the night before, and how much starch Mrs. McGillacutty put into their laundry.

When they were in a bad mood, poor Sarah suffered their presence in the kitchen, as they hovered over her, watching her peeling potatoes and cutting up carrots.

My first encounter with these nuns occurred in September 1955 when I was four and carried screaming into my first day of kindergarten at OLG. I remember that day so vividly. Little kids like me were lined up in long straight lines, ready to enter the squat red brick building that was surrounded by an ominous-looking black iron fence that belonged more in a prison yard than a schoolyard. One half consisted of thick jail-like bars so narrowly spaced a small kitten would get stuck if she had the misfortune to try to slip through. Sharp pointy spikes that resembled spears carried by Crusaders during their bloody wars ran along the top and would one day tragically impale a ten year old boy desperate to flee the priest who was hearing his first confession.

As terrified as I was by that fence, I was even more afraid of my teacher, Sister Immaculate Evangeline-Rosa. Dressed in her long black lacy robes, her head covered by something that looked like a flying saucer, Sister Rosa did not treat screaming children kindly. Her method of control was grabbing the child by the hair and yelling, "Stop it!"

Since I had never been the victim of such barbaric behavior by a stranger, I was so overwhelmed I threw up, spewing the contents of my stomach on Sister Rosa's black shoes and the silky hem of her flowing gown. Fortunately the rosary beads hanging from her thick waist went untouched.

My poor mother who was watching helplessly nearby tried to comfort me, but before I could rush to her side, I was dragged by Sister Rosa into the building where I was handed over to the school nurse, Mrs. Rita McGuire, a short stout lady with enormous breasts and very wide hips. Unlike Sister Rosa she did her best to comfort me while she gently washed my face and hands, and then led me down a long hallway to a room where dozens of kids sat at wooden desks, staring at me in silence.

Sister Rosa stood in the center of the room, chalk in hand, writing the alphabet in large letters across an enormous blackboard.

"Excuse me, Sister," Mrs. McGuire whispered, "But where shall I deposit this child?"

Sister Rosa swung around at the interruption, her silky black robes flapping in the wind like bat wings.

"Over there," she replied, pointing her chalky fingers in the direction of an empty desk near the window.

Mrs. McGuire nodded and led me slowly across the room, but once she released my hand, I quickly panicked and felt like I was being thrown overboard from an ocean liner. I began to bawl again.

A little girl in a green jumper sitting opposite me reached out her hand and then suddenly erupted into tears too. Within minutes everyone in the class with the exception of a few boys and Sister Rosa was crying, screaming, and running amuck.

Kids in other classrooms nearby must have heard the racket, because soon they too joined in. It wasn't until the principal Sister Mary Rogers rushed into our classroom with the pastor, Father O'Brien that everyone calmed down a bit.

"Children," Father O'Brien began, his arms outstretched like Jesus on the cross. "What is going on here? Why such noise? This is your first day of school. You must behave now. If you cry like babies, God will be very unhappy, and we don't want God to be unhappy, do we?"

A few kids shook their heads, terrified, while others sat staring into space swallowing snot and leftover tears.

Sister Mary Rogers thanked Father O'Brien for his wise words, and recited a Hail Mary as soon as quiet descended upon the room.

"I'm sure everything is under control now," Sister Rogers said to Sister Rosa as she exited with the pastor. "You may resume teaching now."

Sister Rosa nodded, picked up her chalk, and stood facing us.

"Class, we will now begin to learn the alphabet. Sit up straight and pay attention. Your education has begun."

Later that afternoon my mother was waiting for me as the dismissal bell rang and I was let free.

I ran to her and buried my head in her lap on the verge of tears again.

As we made our way slowly past the school, my mother saw a Mr. Softie ice cream truck parked nearby. A merry jingle was playing loudly from inside. My mother took hold of my hand, led me over, and then bought me a vanilla ice cream cone with chocolate sprinkles.

Although it had been an extremely difficult day, I had to admit it ended well.

Unfortunately, as the school year unfolded my terror and confusion only increased. I was convinced Sister Rosa hated me for throwing up on her ugly shoes and crying like a baby that first day of kindergarten.

I tried to be good, but Sister Rosa was always finding fault with me. One late afternoon in September during recess period I sat happily coloring a rabbit blue in my favorite coloring book. I chose blue because it was my favorite color. Imagine how surprised I was when Sister Rosa snatched up my picture and held it up to the class.

"This is wrong," she declared, glaring at me. "A rabbit should be colored brown or white. Not blue. There are no blue rabbits. You must observe the world carefully if you are to become an artist."

Startled by the attack and too inarticulate to argue there were no rabbits in Hoboken to observe--all I could do was burst into tears again. This enraged Sister Rosa.

She snatched up my coloring book, tore it in half, and ordered me to sit in a corner in the rear of the room. Several kids in the class began to laugh and I was horrified when a boy named Arthur hit me with a wet spitball when Sister Rosa wasn't looking.

For the remainder of the afternoon I sat with my head down, my stomach in knots, and my confidence shattered. Slowly but surely my brain was being poisoned in Sister Rosa's kindergarten.

That night even a vanilla ice cream cone could not have lifted my spirits. I was much too young to conceive this but years later I realized how the joy and innocence of childhood were destroyed in this god-awful process of attaining a human education under the direction of warped and stupid people.

Nevertheless, like most kids as time passed, I became more resilient and learned to adapt. Besides, something exciting was always happening in my neighborhood and I learned to focus on that. Gazing down at the street from my fourth floor window I saw fist fights, stick ball games, fire trucks racing up narrow streets with their sirens blasting so loud they could wake the dead, and cops raiding the local gambling hall, the Spot Tavern.

One night there was a shoot out between two Puerto Rican gangs and I watched in awe and horror as I saw a man covered in blood collapse onto the sidewalk in front of our building. Eventually I realized this too was all part of my human education. My journey into so-called adulthood had begun.

Today thanks to gentrification and the absurdly high rents of New York City, Hoboken has become an upper class Manhattan with beautiful old brownstones restored to perfection, and old garment and textile factories converted into million dollar condos overlooking the New York City skyline.

In the 1950s, however, most people in the city lived in walk-ups and their kids played games like *Tops* on filthy sidewalks during long, hot summers. Since few people could afford air-conditioning, families gathered on stoops and front steps fanning themselves with the Daily News to keep the flies and heat away.

Gossiping about neighbors was a favorite pastime, especially when it came to the Reilly family—Frank, Margaret, and Katy, who lived in a flat one flight above us.

Everyone sympathized with Margaret, the wife, but no one liked Reilly. He was a silent, morose man who worked as a night watchman down in the Maxwell House Coffee Plant on Hudson Street. He was forever coming home drunk in the dead of the night, waking everyone up and sending tremors through the house as he staggered his bone-thin body up the winding, narrow staircase.

For years, I lived in mortal terror of the man. A six foot, one hundred pound Irishman with flaming red hair, beet-red skin, and wild, blood-shot eyes, he was the leading character in all my childhood nightmares. Perpetually tottering, he seemed always on the bloody verge of destruction. In my worst moments I'd see him tumbling down the stairs backwards and crashing through the milky glass pane of our front door like some terrible ogre, his big head split from end to end.

For some ungodly reason, which I could never understand, my mother seemed to enjoy watching Reilly's worse behavior. Every time she heard him stumbling along, even in the dead of the night when she was already tucked comfortably in her bed, she'd jump up and rush through the dark cold rooms until she arrived at the front door, her right eye twitching with anticipation as she knelt down and peeked out the door's small keyhole.

Blow by blow as the action unfolded she'd fill me in on all the awful details. Reilly was down on his hands and knees trying to crawl up the stairs to his apartment; Margaret was there by his side trying her best to stand him up; two burly cops had arrived on the scene and were dragging Reilly to his feet as he swung at them and cursed; Katy, the poor daughter, was watching from the landing, weeping and wailing as her drunken father was led away and placed in the paddy wagon.

My mother would get so excited narrating the continuing adventures of the Reilly family that she'd even clean out the keyhole with a Q-tip dipped in rubbing alcohol just to make sure she didn't miss anything.

Her heart broke on the day she learned that Reilly had died when he lunged out of O'Casey Saloon one cold night in late December dead drunk and was hit by a dump truck with a broken front head light. Poor Margaret was grief stricken until she began an affair with her life insurance agent a few months after her husband was six-feet under. Without a father or mother in charge, Katy, the daughter, began dating a drop-out from Demarest High School who was known to sell drugs on Observer Highway. She soon got pregnant, quit school, and wound up marrying the cop who delivered her baby when her water broke while she was shopping for Bayer Aspirin in the Acme supermarket.

After the Reilly family was gone and their apartment became empty, my mother turned her keyhole obsession toward another target.

Mary Maloney, an elderly woman, who suffered from dementia, moved into the building, and to everyone's surprise and dismay, quickly became the new janitor. She was forever wandering the halls mumbling to herself as she searched high and low for hidden mice and her dead husband, Harold, whom she believed was lost somewhere in the building.

In return for her labors of hauling out the garbage from the back cellar and mopping the hallway floors once a week, she was given a three room flat on the first floor at half rent.

We'd see her everyday as we trudged up and down the stairs since she kept her front door always open a crack. My mother claimed this was Mary's way of letting Harold know he was still welcome even if he were dead.

Other tenants thought differently.

"She does it to let out the stink," they'd say, joking that they had to hold their noses every time they went by her door.

There was a terrible stink to Mary's flat. It came from all the dirty mops, rags, and filthy pails she used for cleaning the halls. She kept them lined up against her bedroom wall where she'd sit for hours mumbling in the gloomy darkness.

Since everyone felt sorry for Mary, however, no one reported her to the landlord, Mr. Twiddle, an unpleasant man who smelled of garlic and was known for grabbing women's behinds whenever he got the chance.

Some days when I came home from school in the late afternoon and saw Mary down on her hands and knees among the filthy soap bubbles I got really sad.

I cheered up, however, on that unforgettable day when the two mysterious women arrived.

They moved into the five-room apartment directly above us— Edna, a pleasant face buxom lady in her early forties who, we soon learned, wore see-thru blouses and long flowery kimonos that opened to the waist, and Dorothy, a tall, blonde in her early twenties who, it was rumored, sang, and danced in exotic nightclubs in New York City and was once engaged to a gangster on death row.

On the morning of their arrival my mother, hearing excitement taking place in the hallway, dashed to the keyhole, providing me with one of the finest play by plays ever.

I learned that both women spoke a foreign language, wrapped their hair in exotic multicolored scarves, drank white wine, and carried weird looking statues of fat men sitting cross-legged and naked atop immense pillows.

From squatting so long, my mother's right leg fell asleep, so fortunately she had to relinquish her spot at the peephole which I quickly took over.

I knelt down, pressed my right eye up to the keyhole and stared. At first all I saw was my eyelash, but after blinking a few times I focused in on the two women.

They were standing a few feet from my door, facing one another, their hands resting atop each other's shoulders. Then all at once they both leaned forward and kissed. A long, lingering kiss, smack on the lips. Just like that.

I was so shocked, I almost fell over. I couldn't say a word. I simply hung onto the keyhole as if it were a life preserver. Never before in my life—eight years to be exact—had I seen two women kiss like that. I felt like I was going down in an Up elevator at breakneck speed. (Remember this was in the early 1950s America.)

Unlike my schooling at OLG in Sister Rosa's class, this day was the beginning of my real human education. From that moment on, Edna and Dorothy became my obsession. Every time I heard their door slam shut and their feet tapping down the hallway, I long to encounter them. I was more than curious to know everything about these unusual women.

When I did see them in the hallway, I was too shy and tongue-tied to say a word. Compared to all the dull housewives in the neighborhood who spent their lives hanging laundry from clothes lines and screaming at their bratty kids, Edna and Dorothy were like creatures from another planet.

Especially Dorothy, who within only a few short weeks had captured my heart by becoming the talk of the building, the scandal of the whole neighborhood. Night after night I would lie in my bed, picturing her in the room above me smoking cigarettes as she tiptoed around in her open kimono, speaking French, kissing Edna, and crying a little over her dead fiancé whom I picture as Jimmy Cagney.

Why someone as fascinating as Dorothy could inspire so much gossip among the neighborhood women was something I couldn't figure out, but there was no question she became the talk of the town.

"If only the two of them weren't that obvious," Mrs. McCarthy, who lived on the top floor, said to my mother in the laundry room one day.

"If only they didn't flaunt their *aberration* so much. I mean, you would think *those people* would at least know how to use a little discretion."

"What is she talking about?" I asked, staring up at Mrs. McCarthy.

"None of your business," my mother said, shoving me away. "Children should be seen and not heard. Now go play."

Unfortunately, that was the way parents thought in the 50s and there wasn't much I could do about it. I had to wait another year to learn about sex and its many variations from one of my classmates, a girl named Barbara, whom all the boys really seemed to like and who got pregnant in the second year of high school.

As for Dorothy and Edna, I have no idea what happened to them. All I know is that one day I came home from school and saw them driving away in a big moving van. They didn't even wave good-bye.

CHAPTER TWO

Relativity

Normal is boring. Weird is wonderful. Unknown Author

I SPENT A LOT of time after that in my secret hideway: the fire escape outside our kitchen window. I would sit there with my pad and pencil, jotting down thoughts about the world going on around me. As I grew older, I liked describing the various people in my world: neighbors like Crumb Bum Bobbie who worked for the Salvation Army while collecting bets for the illegal local numbers racket. And teachers like Sister Ellen who taught my third grade class.

Not only did she have exactly the kind of eyes I wanted—sapphire blue flecked with hints of purple—she also had the kind of voice I wanted: soft, low, and lilting like notes from a toy xylophone.

It was like no other voice I had ever heard in my life. Sweet and heavenly it was, certainly nothing like my mother's, which my father once described as being similar to a gasoline explosion.

Sister Ellen belonged to an entirely different universe. She was the teacher who introduced me to books and the joy of reading. The only book I can remember in my home was an old medical book that my mother kept on a dusty shelf in the kitchen next to the tea and coffee canisters. It showed grisly colored photos of tangled intestines, swollen bladders, and enlarged livers.

The day Sister Ellen took our class to the Hoboken library was the day my love affair with reading and books began.

I had never been inside a library before so I was surprised when I saw a large torpedo shell encased in glass in the lobby. Looking back I now think this was an educational exhibit meant to remind people suffering from early dementia that World War II had actually taken place, or perhaps it was there to entice kids to learn about history.

However, most of the boys in the class that day were more interested in the torpedo than the books around them, and so Sister Ellen had a hard time trying to stop them from climbing on top of the display case and trying to open it.

I was overwhelmed by the overflowing shelves and spacious rooms filled with beautiful paintings, colorful maps, and rows of thick books. I remember Sister Ellen saying that "*if one were to read all those books, one would become really smart.*"

Since I always believed I was dumb—fractions and long division were beyond me—I was now determined to read everything I could lay my hands on and become smart.

The first book that caught my eye was "***Insights into Reincarnation.***" I had no idea what **reincarnation** was, and I had only a vague notion of what **insight** meant, but it was a beautiful book: black leather with gold trim and it felt wonderful in my hands and smelled divine.

I suspect that if Sister Ellen saw the title she might have objected since the Catholic Church was not keen on introducing little kids to anything except the gospels and the Baltimore Catechism, but maybe because Sister Ellen wanted to take us to a library, I misjudged her.

Although I didn't understand a word of that book as I sat alone reading it, I found the experience so pleasurable it triggered something inside of me. Books and poetry became my passion and set the tone for my life forward.

Years later in high school I would sit for hours savoring the romantic poems of Wordsworth, Keats and Shelley. Poems like *Ode to Immortality*, *To Autumn*, *Ozymandias*, and *To a Skylark*.

In some mysterious way I suppose I was getting ready for the man who would one day walk into my life carrying a big stack of books and reciting poem after poem from the depths of his prodigious memory with a smile and a charming twinkle in his blue eyes.

But that was still years away and in 1958 I was just a little kid who believed in Santa Claus, the tooth fairy, and the mysterious power of my mother to read minds and see what was happening behind her.

Like a lot of children in those days I got sick from the whooping cough, the German measles, the Hong Kong flu, chicken pox, Mumps, appendicitis, Scarlet Fever, and the worse case of colitis you can ever imagine. Since my father, Mick, was working all the time it was my mother who was home all day taking care of me."

"Your father is never here to help," she would complain. "He's out gallivanting while I'm here slaving away."

The word *Gallivanting* was a mystery to me. I thought it meant working hard since Mick worked over 40 hours a week as a fireman and then moonlighted on the side in various jobs to earn extra money. He drove trucks, painted houses, bartended in the Spot Tavern, and helped out in Boswell's funeral home carrying in the caskets and setting up the viewing rooms.

My mother, however, insisted he was spending his time fooling around with the "blond tomato."

I had no idea what she was talking about since all the tomatoes I saw were red in salads.

I also couldn't understand why my mother was always mad at my father whom she called *Shitface* and *Dirty Bastard*."

Imagine my surprise then when I woke one night and saw my mother down on her knees praying for him.

It was the night of the Burlington Rubber Factory fire on Observer Highway and outside our window, high above the wail of screeching fire trucks and roaring ambulances, flashes of bright red and orange flames were shooting across the sky, sending mountains of smoke through the mile-square city.

"My poor Louie," she cried. "My darling husband."

I was baffled. Never in my life had I heard my mother call my father *her darling husband.*

"What going on, Ma? I asked, seeing her prostrate on the floor of our living room.

"Oh, pray for your poor father, she wailed. " There's a terrible fire in town and I'm afraid he may be killed."

"Killed? How?"

I didn't understand. I was so frightened I could barely speak.

"If the building collapses and he falls into the fire, they'll never find his body. He'll be nothing but teeth and ashes. That's all we will have left of him. Teeth and ashes."

Terrorized, I pictured my father as a giant molar.

"Oh, if only I could be there with him," she said, shaking her head sadly. If only I could see him one more time before he dies."

"Let's go then," I begged, tears streaming down my cheeks. "I want to see him one more time too."

She turned and looked at me, a faint smile lighting her face.

"Should we? It's a school night, you know. You should be in bed. People will say I'm a bad mother."

How my mother could think of school at a time like this was beyond me, but I must confess that as the two of us headed out the door, dressed hastily in our long, wool coats, hats and fur-lined boots, I did begin to worry what we might encounter on that terrible night.

The Burlington Rubber Factory was clear across town, almost ten blocks away from Fourth and Adams Street and it was a windy bitter cold night, but as we dashed across icy pavements, our arms locked firmly together like trusty conspirators, we hardly noticed the cold. Both of us were too caught up in our own fantasies to consider what lay ahead.

"I'm sure the priest is there and will administer the last rites if necessary," my mother declared, wiping my running nose with the tip of her grey mitten. "It will probably be Father Donnelly or Father Burke. Father Fitzgerald is too old to be out on a night like this, God help him. Why this wind alone would kill the old bugger in the blink of an eye."

We were fast approaching the scene of the fire. Police cars, fire trucks, and emergency vehicles raced past us, their flashing, whirling red lights casting long blood shadows far into the smoky darkness.

My eyes were burning with soot and floating ash, and I began to gag from fumes of thick poisonous smoke.

And then before I knew what was happening, I was high in the air.

Looking down all I could see was the sharp peak and wide sloping brim of a fireman's helmet.

"Charlie," I heard my mother shout. "Thank God you're working. Have you seen Louie? Is he dead or alive or what?"

"Helen, calm down. Louie is fine. He's around here somewhere."

Uncle Charlie planted a kiss on my nose and placed me back on the ground where I became entangled in the wet folds of his smoke-drenched raincoat.

"Are you sure he's not hurt?" my mother wailed again, peering into the smoky darkness.

"I'm sure Louie is fine. You're going to frighten Patsy, so calm down. Everything is good, trust me. Now I have to get back to work."

Uncle Charlie said good-bye, patted me on the head, and hurried away.

Of all the firemen I saw that night my father was the only one who was smoking a cigarette when we finally spotted him, strolling casually across the narrow stone bridge connecting the North and South sections of the rubber factory.

"Look, Patsy," my mother screamed, pointing. "It's your father. The stinker is alive after all."

She genuflected, and made the sign of the cross quickly across her body.

For the first time in my life, I began to wonder if my mother was indeed a little strange as I heard some people say.

At night when other kids my age were being read *Little Red Riding Hood* and *Snow White and the Seven Dwarfs*, my mother read me headlines from the Daily News and the New York Post. **Attractive Blond Slashed in Alleyway; Mother of Nine Raped in Laundromat.**

I guess this was her way of educating me about life while expanding my vocabulary. She was convinced the world was a dangerous place, and perverts were everywhere.

On days when my mother and I ventured into the small park on Fourth and Willow Street in the late afternoon she made sure I didn't wander far away. While other kids climbed the monkey bars and rode the merry-go-round in the children's sandlot, I had to sit on a bench with her to remain safe."

My mother truly believed anyone who frequented a park—with the exception of herself and a few lady friends—was a social misfit, deranged and dangerous. She was always on the lookout for old men in long raincoats lurking behind garbage cans and trees. She refused to allow me to visit the park toilet by myself even when I desperately needed to go. Drinking at water fonts was also forbidden since she was convinced sex perverts used them for urinals.

One hot summer afternoon when most of the other kids in the park were roller-skating, riding their bikes, and playing tag, I sat bored and restless on a hard bench wedged between my mother and her two friends, Mrs. Mueller and Mrs. Dugan who talked nonstop about their good-for-nothing husbands and their snotty, ungrateful children.

My only entertainment was watching the pigeons who paraded back and forth atop the memorial statue of the *Hoboken Fireman* who died rescuing an infant from a burning apartment.

Over seven feet high and surrounded by a spiked iron fence, the *Hoboken Fireman* was an awesome sight, even to child. He stood dead center in the park, fixed in the eternal pose of a fearless rescuer: head high, eyes blazing, arms clutching the limp body of an infant carried from a blazing tenement.

Local politicians proudly insisted he was the city's only official monument; taxpayers complained he was a health menace and a danger to children who scaled over the fence and climbed his immense torso.

Every year workmen would arrive in the park with buckets of disinfectants to clean him up and restore the tarnished brass plaque beneath his left boot. For a little while he glowed and sparkled until the pigeons returned and resumed their relentless bombing attacks.

On the day Mrs. O'Casey wandered into the park and sat down on the empty bench across from us, the fireman was covered in pigeon poop, soot and green mold.

Like the statue, Mrs. O'Casey didn't look so good either. She was so thin she resembled a walking skeleton. She sat upright, staring straight ahead. Her eyes were yellow, bulging, and lake-large. Her head resembled the skull of a new born baby: bald with just a few flaky wisps of white snow that a soft breeze might blow away.

She was the oddest person I ever saw. When she stood to remove her sweater, her shoulders stuck out like angel wings.

I began to imagine she had just arrived from heaven and was waiting for God to help her fly away.

"Mama," I asked. "Can I go and talk with that lady over there. She looks lonely."

"What lady?" She glanced around as Mrs. Mueller and Mrs. Dugan chatted on.

I pointed to the bench.

My mother leaned forward and stared.

"No," she whispered "That woman is sick. Leave her alone. Mind your own business."

"But she looks so sad."

"Well, there's nothing you can do about that."

"I can talk to her."

"No, you can't. I feel sorry for the poor woman too. But you can't just go up to strangers and begin talking to them."

"Why not?" I asked.

"Because . . . ."

"Because why?"

"Because I'm your mother and I'm telling you not to."

Mrs. Mueller and Mrs. Dugan stopped talking and looked at me.

"What's going on, Helen?" Mrs. Dugan asked with a smile. "Is Patsy being a little brat again?"

"No," my mother replied. "She just feels sorry for that woman sitting over there who looks sick. She wants to talk to her."

I wanted to punch Mrs. Dugan. She was mean. I hadn't done anything and she called me a brat.

Mrs. Mueller stood up and took a closer look at the woman.

"Why, that's Mrs. O'Casey. She used to live across from me on Jefferson Street. I haven't seen her in a long time. I know her husband died a few years back. She moved after that. God, she does look sick, doesn't she?"

"Yes," Mrs. Dugan agreed. "I wonder what's wrong with her."

"Cancer, probably. Let's go see."

Mrs. O'Casey seemed a little confused and uncomfortable when Mrs. Dugan and Mrs. Mueller descended on her, sat down, and began chatting away.

I started thinking maybe my mother was right and it was wrong to just bother someone when they wanted to be alone.

I felt better, however, when Mrs. O'Casey finally looked over at me and waved.

I waved back.

My mother saw what was happening, took me by the hand, and led me over to her.

"Mrs. Mueller told me you were neighbors. I'm her friend, Helen, and this is my daughter, Patsy. We just want to say hello. We hope we're not disturbing you?"

"Not at all," Mrs. O'Casey replied, smiling at me. "I love children and I can tell Patsy is a very sweet and smart little girl."

She winked at me. Then she stood up slowly and gently patted me on the head.

"Sorry, ladies, but I'm just a little tired, and I have to say good-bye now. It was lovely meeting you all."

Before anyone could reply, Mrs. O'Casey slipped away.

That was the last time I saw her.

But that brief encounter was one more step up the ladder of my human education. I realized then that being sick and being alone were terrible things that could happen to anyone at any time.

CHAPTER THREE

The Cosmic Dance: Flux, Motion, Change

Everyone sees a different truth because everyone is creating what they see. P. Jordan

AS I GOT a little older I grew a lot closer to my father. The little things he did—his world was so different from my mother's –fascinated me. I especially liked to watch him shave in the morning. He'd stand over the kitchen sink, stirring the sweet smelling shaving soap in the old jam jar and then brush it onto his face with quick easy strokes. To this day I can still hear the scraping sound the straight- backed razor made against his stubble cheeks and chin as he scratched the foaming soap away.

I also loved seeing him all dressed·up in his fireman's uniform when he left for work in the morning. I was very proud of him since he looked so brave and handsome in his blue jacket and blue hat with the gold badge that shone so brightly in the sunlight.

When my father finished his shift at the fire house, he would go to his other jobs. The poor man worked so hard, but my parents were always short of money and lived from paycheck to paycheck. Firemen in those days were not paid very much and many of them had to moonlight to make a decent living. One of those moonlighting jobs my father had was delivering neighborhood gambling slips to Mike the Barber who ran the local betting network.

Today when gambling is as acceptable as going to church on Sunday since states profit from the taxes collected, people don't remember how dangerous it was back then when betting was considered a crime.

My father wasn't paid much for taking such a big risk. I think he just enjoyed the excitement of dodging the cops and rubbing shoulders with guys like Zoo-Zoo, Joe the Duck and Snot-Nose Tony.

Since Mick wasn't around much during the day, it was my mother who always picked me up from OLG and walked me home. I was surprised one afternoon in late Fall when I saw my father waiting for me outside the school.

"Hi, Baby Doll. Are you happy to see me?"

I nodded as he took me by the hand.

"Would you like to go on a little adventure today?" he asked, as we skipped along.

"Sure, "I replied. "What kind of adventure?"

"A secret mission involving hidden messages that I want you to deliver to our neighbor, Mike the Barber. You like Mike, right?"

"Yes," I said. "He's a nice man and he gives me lemon lollipops sometimes when I walk by his shop with Mommy."

"Is that right? Well, maybe today Mike will give you some more lollipops after you see him and deliver these messages."

"What kind of messages, Daddy?"

"Secret messages with lots of magical numbers, so it's very important that they are delivered safely."

"Why?"

"Because a lot of people have dreamed up these magical numbers, and wait to see what happens to them."

Holding hands, we continued our stroll down Willow Avenue, passing Ryan's Pub on the right and Mary's Florist shop on the left. The air smelled of flowers and beer and I was very happy.

That is until I suddenly realized something was missing in this conversation.

"Does Mommy know about this secret mission?" I asked.

"No, and it's very important you don't tell her."

"Why? Won't she be mad if we don't tell her?"

"Not at all. In fact, some of the messages are from her with numbers she picked all by herself."

"Really?"

"Yes. Trust me, Patsy Doll. She will be very proud of you when she learns her daughter delivered these numbers all by herself. All you have to do is hide them under that school beanie you are wearing and bring them to Mike the Barber without letting anyone else see them. O.K.?"

"O.K."

"Good girl!"

We walked another block before we arrived home. When we entered the vestibule my father made sure no one was watching as he handed me a thick stack of small folded paper.

"Here, Patsy. Stick these under your beanie. Run straight over to the barber shop and when you're sure no one is looking, hand them over to Mike."

I was more than excited. I was elated. I never felt more important in my life.

I took hold of the stack of paper and stashed it under my beanie making sure everything was hidden. Mick gave me a quick kiss and I was on my way.

Mike was ready for me. I saw him peeking out from the front store window. He quickly let me inside. The place was empty. It smelled of cigar smoke and hair tonic.

"Hello, cutie. How's things?"

I glanced around, my eyes falling on his row of red leather barber chairs.

"Can I sit in one of those chairs?" I asked. "I have secret messages I need to deliver."

"Sure, kid. Hop up." I climbed on the middle chair where I could see the red, white and blue barber pole hanging outside the window going round and round.

"What'dja got for me, kid?"

I took off my beanie and handed over the paper.

Mike grabbed the stack, rushed over to a cluttered nearby shelf and deposited the folded slips inside a flower pot that housed a dying sunflower.

"You're a good kid," Mike beamed winking at me. "You done a great job. How about a lemon lollipop?"

Pretty soon I was delivering secret messages not only to Mike the Barber but to Fatsy the Frankfurter Man; Mario the local bread maker, and Angelo who ran Killer Pizza on Fifth and Washington Street.

Everything was fine until the day my beanie blew off in a heavy rain and wind storm and all the slips of paper went flying in every direction into the air.

After that, my father decided my cover was blown and the risk was too great to continue,

My mother, fortunately, never knew what was going on, but one night when she hit the Pick-Three number 913 straight up for 400 bucks, she and my father danced me around the room, covering me with kisses and grateful hugs.

Now, fifty years later I realize my very first job was a numbers runner who managed to outwit the local and federal police from suspecting illegal gambling in the neighborhood.

Maybe it was my experience working as a hard-core numbers runner at such a young age, but as I grew a little older I learned more about people and how to deal with them.

Mr. Sill was the life insurance salesman who came to the house once a month to collect payment on the policy my parents had opened after my brother Jim and I were born. Mr. Sill was an odd-looking little man with a grey wrinkled face covered in coarse, spiky whiskers that reminded me of the Brillo pads my mother kept under the sink in the kitchen.

He dressed in black suits and a long black overcoat that smelled of mothballs and gasoline.

His eyes were strange too. They were yellow and filmy like the bottom of a dirty egg cup that hadn't been properly washed. I didn't like him at all and always felt uncomfortable when he arrived and sat down at the kitchen table, helping himself to the cookies and raisin toast my mother so generously placed before him.

I sat watching him from across the room as I pretended to play at my desk with the pencil sharpener.

He had no table manners at all. In fact, he didn't even wash his hands before eating. I hoped that my mother who was sitting opposite him, drinking tea, would not eat anything on that table after he had touched it.

I was surprised how quiet my mother was around him. I thought she was being extra polite, hoping he wouldn't object when she told him she couldn't pay that month's insurance bill.

Money was always tight in our house and my parents sometimes had to take out loans from a finance company to keep afloat.

After Mr. Sill had eaten all the cookies and bread on his plate, he put on his glasses, leaned back in his chair, and stared at my mother.

"Thank you for breakfast," he said, reaching for her hand. "I suppose we have to get down to business now but first I would like to confess I find you a very attractive comely woman."

I had no idea what the word *comely* meant, but I gathered it wasn't a compliment since my mother gave him a dirty look, stood up and quickly began clearing the table.

Once my mother was safely in the kitchen, Mr. Sill sighed and gazed around the room. When his fishy eyes fell on me, he began to laugh.

"Well, look who's been hiding without saying hello. Come and give Uncle Sill a big kiss."

I stared at him in silence.

"Are you deaf, sweetie? I said come over here and give your uncle a nice big kiss."

"No," I said, shaking my head.

"Why not?' he pouted.

"Because you're not my uncle."

"No, but I'm still a nice man and I have something pretty little girls like you would like."

He reached into his pocket and pulled out a package of peppermint Life Savers."

"Here, have one."

"No. I don't like peppermint. It tastes like medicine."

"Really? Well, next time I'll bring you some chocolate."

"I don't like chocolate either."

"Are you sure? Everyone likes chocolate."

"Well, I don't," I replied, hoping he would go away.

"Would you like to come and sit on my lap," he asked. "Maybe then you can tell me what you do like."

His teeth were yellow and crooked like his face. He sat down, spreading his legs apart. Then he unbuttoned his long black overcoat and held it open beckoning me forward.

His pants smelled of wet basements and moldy cheese.

"Mommy," I called, looking away." Mommy, come here."

She rushed out of the kitchen.

"What? What's going on?"

She looked at me and then at Mr. Sill.

He began to cough, pulling a large white cotton handkerchief from his jacket pocket. He spit into it several times.

"Sorry," he said. "Pretty dusty in here and I guess I'm allergic to dust."

"My home is not dusty," my mother said. "Perhaps you should leave if you think that."

"Well, I do need some fresh air."

"He smells," I announced to my mother, as he turned away, gathering up his pens, papers, and satchel.

My mother nodded, placing her hand over my mouth as Mr. Sill headed for the door.

"I'll send you this month's bill in the mail," he said. "Obviously, **Home Life** expects your payment on time."

Once the door was shut and Mr. Sill was safely on his way, my mother and I began to laugh.

"You are naughty," she said, pitching my cheek. "But you're smart too. You can spot a pervert from a mile away just like me."

In celebration of our newly found affinity, we left the apartment hand in hand on our way to the local ice cream shop.

CHAPTER FOUR

Aberrant Variables in Closed Systems

The universe is a web of interconnected and inseparable energy patterns. Barbara Brennan

IN THE 1950S the kids in grammar school were far more innocent than the kids today. No one could imagine bringing a gun to school, shooting the teacher because of a bad grade, or selling drugs in the cafeteria during lunch hour.

If you failed your lessons, you were left back and had to repeat the entire year all over again while your smarter friends moved on and left you behind. Teachers were the final authority and school principals were always given the highest respect.

A problem student was labeled a misfit and treated accordingly. Freddie Gasholinski, a kid in my sixth grade class, who had been left behind three times, was a perfect example of this. He was expelled from Our lady of Grace after hurling a brick from the school roof that just missed decapitating Sister Rita as she was feeding a pool of marbled pigeons in the dusty courtyard.

Sadly, Freddie never fit in. He was 6 foot 4 inches tall in the sixth grade and weighed over 200 pounds. His face was pocket-marked with pimples and his breath smelled like road kill. He had no friends, and everyone was afraid of him including his teachers.

By the time Freddie was 18 he was a convicted felon, found guilty of armed robbery at a local gas station, and sentenced to ten years in prison. Today a kid like Freddie would be diagnosed as socially challenged and placed in a special education class where he would eventually graduate with honors. A year later he would attend college majoring in *remedial everything* and then land a city job in Urban planning where he would be in charge of new building construction. *Times change* is an understatement, I think.

Unlike poor Freddie I began to thrive by the time I reached sixth grade.

Maybe that was because my teacher was not a nun but a woman everyone knew from the neighborhood.

Mrs Heany was married with two kids and lived in a four story walk up over Henry's Candy shop on the corner of Jefferson and Fifth Street. Her husband worked in the sanitation department riding the dump truck through town.

He seemed like a friendly guy since he always waved at people as he hung off the back of the truck in his dirty overalls and heavy black gloves.

They made an odd couple since Mrs. Heany never looked dirty and was always reserved and proper in public. She wore her hair in a big neat bun that sat primly on the top of her head, and she dressed like it was Sunday morning and she was on her way to church.

I think some women were jealous of her since her skirts were made of real wool and theirs were cheap polyester from Mickey Finn's department store.

Mrs. Heany's kids went to OLG and so working there was easy for her. Like most women at that time, she never attended college or attained any academic degrees, but she knew how to handle a roomful of rambunctious kids. The school hired her because it desperately needed teachers to manage the baby boom that sprang up after the war.

Being assigned to her class was a lot better than winding up in Mrs. Sullivan's class because Mrs. Sullivan cried all the time. Her six year old daughter had died from leukemia and shortly thereafter her husband took off with his secretary. She was a terrible teacher and a severely depressed woman who should never have been hired.

Mrs. Heany was really good at teaching everything except arithmetic. She loved drawing columns of numbers across the blackboard and then handing the chalk to some unsuspecting student, like me, to find the answers.

I'd stand there holding the chalk, pretending I was deep in thought when all I was doing was looking at Mrs. Heany's black leather shoes and admiring how they shone under the florescent lights.

Unlike the nuns Mrs. Healy was very patient. She never screamed or smacked us on the back of the head, and when I got the answer wrong, which was 95 percent of the time, she told me to sit down and try harder next time.

I think if Mrs. Healy had been good at arithmetic herself or shown us an easier way of working with numbers I would have made some progress. But unfortunately, that never happened and so by the time I was in high school and had to study algebra, geometry, and trigonometry I was a hopeless case. When testing time arrived, I would go to church and pray to St Jude, the patron of Hopeless Cases.

Saint Jude. Are you listening? This is me. Patsy. Please help me to pass this upcoming Algebra test. I promise I will donate two bucks to the starving kids in Africa and the homeless orphans in Ethiopia if I get anything over 70%.

To this day I believe it was my fear of failing math that sustained my religious faith all through grammar school.

Miss Kale, the Mathematics teacher at Sacred Heart Academy, an all-girl preparatory high school located on seventh and Washington Street in Hoboken, which I attended from 1964 to 1969, tried her best to teach me but failed miserably. Her lectures about the beautiful logic and breathtaking symmetries of an orderly numerical universe, fell on deaf ears.

It was the 1960s and the universe looked anything but logical and orderly. John F. Kennedy, our beloved president, was shot dead before our eyes as he rode in a motorcade through Dallas; Martin Luther King was gunned down on a balcony in Alabama; bloody violent riots were taking place in cities across the nation, and young men were dying by the thousands in Vietnam.

Meanwhile back in Hoboken, teenagers like me were watching the Beatles on the Ed Sullivan Show and smoking pot after school in Kelly's Hideway on Garden street.

It was hard to relate to Miss Kale, a nerd, who lived with her sick mother in a Newark tenement, and who, no doubt, dreamed of polygons, complimentary angles, diagonals, and lovely logarithms at night.

I always sat in the back of her classroom next to the window where I could look up at the blue sky and wonder where all the airplanes flying overhead were going and what the passengers inside were doing. I liked to imagine I was one of those passengers on my way to Paris to open a café-bookshop on the Champ Elysee where I would live happily ever after with a French poodle and a handsome husband named Antoine.

Since Miss Kale knew I was hopeless when it came to numbers and abstract calculations, she rarely called on me to answer a question or explain a theorem.

I was convinced it was only because of Saint Jude's intercession that I finally passed the course. I guess it also helped that I was getting high grades in all my other subjects and never made nasty comments about her clothes and hair like some other girls in her class did.

Miss Kale was a smart lady, but I still felt sorry for her. I couldn't imagine what it must have been like to live with a sick mother in Newark and not have a lover or poodle in Paris.

My favorite course at Sacred Heart was *Introduction to Philosophy* taught by Mr. Giorgio, a thin Philippine man who spoke in whispers and puffed on Camel cigarettes after every class in the alleyway behind the building.

His hair was jet black and he had a nervous habit of running his chalk-stained hands through it while lecturing on the death of Socrates or Plato's *Allegory of the Cave.* I always sat in the front row mesmerized by the way he spoke without notes. He would pace back and forth, describing in vivid detail how Socrates bravely drank the hemlock poison as a way of defying the authorities who sentenced him to death on false charges of corrupting the youth of his day.

Mr. G, as we called him, insisted Socrates was condemned because he was a *gadfly*, a man who was unafraid of questioning the status quo and criticizing those in power.

That was the first time I ever heard the word, *gadfly*, and I immediately incorporated it into my limited vocabulary by using it every chance I got.

Since I always paid attention in Mr. G's class, I learned about Aristotle, Kant, Descartes, Nietzsche, Hume, Sartre, and my favorite writer and philosopher Albert Camus. I read everything I could find about French existentialism, free will, and nihilism.

Looking back I think Mr. G's class was getting me ready for all the philosophy and ethics classes I would take as a freshman at St. Peter's College, a Jesuit institution on Kennedy Blvd. in Jersey City. The college was known for its high academic standards and its emphasis on the Humanities.

I was thrilled when I received the acceptance letter in the mail.

My brother Jim, who was four years older than I, was the first person in the family to go to college. He became a member of the Argus Eyes, the theatre club, playing leading roles like *Hero* in *A Funny Thing Happened on the Way to the Forum* and *Peter* in Edward Albee's *The Zoo Story*.

I was very proud of my brother and deeply wanted to be like him. I had no idea how one day a suggestion of his would change my entire life.

CHAPTER FIVE

The Law of Attraction

*I like dreamin' cause dreamin' can
make you mine. Kenny Nolan*

JIM GRADUATED FROM St. Peter's in 1969, the year I entered as a freshman.

Since my dream was to operate a bookstore one day, I decided to major in English and American Literature.

I had been prepared to take a French Literature class for six weeks, beginning in early June and ending in mid July, but when it came time to register, I learned the class had been cancelled for lack of enrollment.

"Why not take Dr. Flinn's British and Continental Literature class?" Jim suggested when he saw how disappointed I was over the cancellation. "I heard he's a really good teacher, but a tough grader, so be prepared."

Prepared was the last thing I was when Dr. Eugene C. Flinn strolled through the classroom door that night in early spring 1970. He was dressed in orange socks, summer sandals, and red plaid Scottish trousers. He wore a nicely trimmed reddish beard and his hair was curly and as wild as a bird's nest in late summer.

He was carrying at least twenty paperbacks. I remember specifically Oscar Williams' *Anthology of Poetry* and Max Frisch's *I'm Not Stiller*. For some reason the title of Frisch's book intrigued me. Years later I would find out why.

"Are you ready for lots of reading and discussion?" he asked, eyeing the startled faces of each student.

There were twenty of us. Ten women and ten men who like me sat quietly, listening to his every word.

"Reading and thinking are the best things for a growing brain," he smiled. "If you do that all your life, you will be among the intellectual elite with the rare ability to distinguish truth from horseshit."

He laughed, spreading the paperbacks across his desk.

"*Sergeant's Musgrave's Dance* by John Arden is a play about the evils and absurdities of war," he said. "That topic never goes out of style. While Max Frisch's *I'm Not Stiller* is an intriguing tale of a man who refuses to accept the limited concept of *self identity* other people have given him."

"Frisch, a Swiss novelist known for his. . . ."

I was copying down everything he said as fast as I could in my little blue notebook.

"Joe Orton, best known for his scandalous black comedies *Entertaining Mr. Sloan* and *Loot*, was murdered by his gay lover in 1967. We'll be seeing his play, *What the Butler Saw* at the end of the semester."

I knew then that this course was going to be different from any of the others I had taken at the college. The reading material was controversial and timely and the professor seemed witty and unconventional, a rarity in a conservative Catholic College.

It was a three hour class held twice a week, but that first class and all the others flew by in the blink of an eye. At least that was how it felt to me.

Over the course of the semester Dr. Flinn mentioned the names and locations of several bookstores he enjoyed visiting in New York City. I was fired up to check them out. At the time there were no bookstores in Hoboken and only one in Jersey City.

After each class ended I wanted to talk with Dr. Flinn, but I was a bit shy and didn't want to interrupt his time with other students, so I always just gathered up my books and left the room quietly.

One night, however, I was halfway down the stairs in McNulty Hall when I heard something drop behind me. I looked up and saw Dr. Flinn struggling to retrieve two books that had fallen from his arms. I rushed to his side to help.

When he looked at me, he grinned as if he had planned the whole thing. When our eyes met I experienced something that to this day

I cannot fully explain. Call it déjà vu, but I felt as if I had lived that moment before. It was like a door opening into a room so warm and familiar I could not resist entering.

We stood there on the steps staring at each other and stuttering like awkward teenagers on a first date.

He asked if I were enjoying the class. I could barely speak. I just shook my head and mumbled I loved it.

I was so nervous standing there looking at him I told a lie. I said I had to leave because a friend was waiting for me.

He nodded and thanked me for helping him with his falling books.

I hurried away, confused, unsettled, and strangely elated.

I didn't know it consciously at that time but my life was soon to change in ways I could never have imagined.

After that first conversation on the worn marble steps in the hallway of the old McNulty building, Dr. Flinn and I resumed our separate roles as teacher and student.

Halfway through the semester he assigned everyone in the class a poem to analyze and discuss. I was given Dylan Thomas's *In My Craft and Sullen Art*.

I remember sitting late at night at the kitchen table in our apartment reading the poem aloud with no one to hear me except my dog Sandy, a collie and shepherd mix who was resting at my feet, wagging his tail as I recited every stanza. My mother was in bed and my father was on duty at the fire house.

The late night loneliness of the cold water flat and the fading light of the half moon shining through the window enhanced my melancholy mood, just the right emotion to approach Thomas's poem. I could picture the lovers wrapped in each other's arms, caring not a whit that only a short distance away a poet was struggling to find words to express the inexpressible.

I began enjoying *In My Craft and Sullen Art* so much, I decided I would read every one of Thomas's poems and his essays too.

When my father learned that I was on my way to New York City to visit some bookshops in Greenwich Village he insisted on driving me there.

"I used to work in the train station on 9th street," he told me. "I know the city like the back of my hand, Patsy doll."

And so we went. Our first stop was the old Strand Bookshop at 821 Broadway. It was packed with shoppers. There were no places to park the old Rambler, so my father waited in the car while I browsed inside. I found two books on the reading list and bought them both.

Although my father was a really smart man, he never had the opportunity to go to college or even to finish high school. I knew he had never been in a bookstore in his life. I was surprised when he offered to help me shop.

"It'll save us time since that list of books you got is pretty long. I'll check out a few places while you're busy here."

Reluctantly, I handed him half the list and he wandered off.

While I was browsing inside *The Perry Street BookMart,* my father was searching for a nearby shop. The first one he saw was *Adult Books and Magazines* on Sixth Street.

He told me later that a young man with long greasy hair who looked as if he hadn't showered in a year was smoking a cigarette behind the check-out desk. I could picture what happened after that.

"Hey kid, can you help me find these books?"

He handed over the list.

Kafka's Letter to his Father; Thomas Mann's Magic Mountain; James Joyce's The Dubliners; Berthold Brecht's The Caucasian Chalk Circle.

The clerk handed back the list and rubbed his nose.

"You're in the wrong place, Mac. We don't sell those kinds of books here."

Apparently, my father did not notice the posters of naked women hanging on the walls, or the shelves of lurid sex toys blatantly for sale near the cash register.

"But these books are for adults, right? The sign outside said *Adult Book Store.*

"Look, Mister, I'm telling you. This ain't the bookstore you're looking for."

He pulled two books from a nearby shelf and thrust them under my father's face.

Blowjobs Unlimited and *Fat-Ass Fannie in the Foxhole.*

"Now do you understand? I ain't selling Jane Austin here."

"That's disgusting," my father said, eyeing the covers on both books, as he backed out of the store. "The cops should know about this place. It's a disgrace."

Over the coming weeks, Mick became more familiar and relaxed in bookstores. I vividly remember one in New Brunswick, right near Rutgers University, where the owner, an elderly man in an old tweed suit and matching vest, sat in a worn leather chair smoking his pipe with his collie dog at his side. From that moment on I always wanted to own a bookstore where I would sit contentedly reading books all day with a loyal dog by my side.

I could tell Mick enjoyed being in that shop and talking to the owner, Mr. Cunningham, who always seemed delighted to hear stories about the Hoboken Fire department. Mr. Cunningham, who was born in County Mayo, Ireland, kept a bottle of Jamison Irish Whiskey behind the check-out counter and while I roamed through the store, he and Mick enjoyed a shot or two.

I don't know if my father ever finished the book Mr. Cunningham gave him—a biography of Harry Truman, but I was delighted when I saw him reading it at the kitchen table in place of the *Daily News.*

A few days later with some of my new books in hand, I headed for Dr. Flinn's class. I saw him sitting atop his desk chatting with a woman I had never seen before. She certainly wasn't a member of the class and when she spoke I detected a strong Irish accent. My heart fell a little since I immediately thought she was probably his girlfriend.

But I was surprised to see he was staring and smiling at me. I hurried to my desk and after a few minutes more students began to trickle in.

"Class, this is my good friend, Mary Flynn. She is visiting from County Galway, Ireland, and I wanted to show her our campus."

I was surprised and relieved to know she was not his girlfriend. After we welcomed Mary Flynn and she took a seat next to me in the front row, Dr. Flinn called my name.

"Patricia, are you ready to discuss Dylan Thomas's poem *In My Craft and Sullen Art* ?"

"Yes," I said, leaping out of my seat.

I had memorized the short poem, so I needed no book. I took a deep breath and began.

Dr. Flinn was listening carefully and smiling all the time I spoke and when I came to the line about the lovers lying in bed with the full moon raging, I began to blush.

Mary Flynn, meanwhile, was rummaging through her huge pocketbook looking for a Kleenex. A few seconds later she began loudly blowing her nose.

After I finished my presentation, Dr. Flinn congratulated me on doing an excellent job of interpreting the work and analyzing it so well.

I was elated that he liked what I had done. After that night, the rest of the semester seemed to fly by like a dream, and although I attended every class, we never talked again after class.

Maybe it was my Catholic school education or his professionalism that sealed our separate roles as teacher and student, but that was how we behaved.

Even on the final night when the class went to New York City to see Joe Orton's *What the Butler Saw,* and later gathered in Chumley's Pub in the Village for a late snack and discussion, I left for home early without talking privately to Dr. Flinn.

CHAPTER SIX

Parallel Universes and Multiple Realities

I think I can safely say that nobody understands
Quantum Mechanics. Richard P. Feynman

YEARS LATER WHEN we were married, Gene told me how disappointed he was that I had left so soon.

"I wanted so much to see and talk to you that night. I feared I would never see you again once the class was over."

Fate was on our side, however.

Once all the grades had been submitted and the semester was officially over, Dr. Flinn decided to invite the entire class to his apartment on Bentley Ave. in Jersey City to celebrate his birthday.

The party was to begin around 7 p.m. and my father offered to drive me there.

"Take your time and have fun," he said, as he parked the old Rambler in front of the building.

Give me a call when you're ready to leave."

I waved good-bye and headed for the entrance door.

I was expecting to see Dr. Flinn when I rang the bell, but I was surprised when a teenage girl with long blond hair swung open the door and immediately asked who I was.

"I'm one of Dr. Flinn's students. He invited the class to a party tonight for his birthday."

"I know," she said with a bored shrug. "My father's in the living room."

I was stunned. I had no idea he was married.

As soon as Dr. Flinn saw me, he jogged over to greet me. He looked very handsome in his dark blue turtle neck and black pants that fit his tall lean frame perfectly.

"Happy birthday," I said, handing him the small present I had bought and the poem I had written for him.

He thanked me several times and began reading the poem. It was about a Ferris wheel in a deserted amusement park that spins for eternity.

"I love it," he said. "You must keep writing."

Even though the room was filled with students and some of his friends, Dr. Flinn continued to chat with me.

Eventually someone turned off the lights and a man named Paul came marching out of the small kitchen carrying a flaming birthday cake. Paul, who would later play such an important role in our lives, was Dr. Flinn's closest friend. He was a superb cook and baker and while everyone sang Happy Birthday, he cut slices of cake and handed them out.

There were about thirty people there, students from the class, neighbors, and several men who appeared to be close friends of Dr. Flinn. I kept looking around wondering where Mrs. Flinn was, but there was no sign of her.

I spent most of the night chatting with my friends from class, several of whom were getting tipsy after drinking generous amounts of cold Sangria and sparkling champagne. Dr. Flinn's apartment was sparse in furniture but overflowing with books, magazines and framed photographs. As I wandered around the rooms, curious as a straying cat, I learned Dr. Flinn had taken these photos. Many of them were shots of people caught unexpectedly by the camera. A woman bathing her feet in the Fontana delle Tartarughe in Rome; an elderly man smoking a cigar on a park bench in Central Park; a young couple kissing beneath an ancient redwood in California on a summer day.

I was intrigued by Dr. Flinn's keen eye for detail and appreciation for life's simple moments. I loved looking at all his books-literature, history, art, philosophy, an amazing collection of biographies. Several large clocks with waving brass pendulums dotted the cream colored walls and chimed on the half hour.

The flat in Hoboken where I lived had only three small windows, but this apartment had windows that reached from floor to ceiling. It was easy to imagine this cozy space flooded with light and fresh air on warm summer days.

Around 10 that evening, people began to leave and Dr. Flinn stood at the door thanking everyone from coming to his party and wishing them well.

I found my jacket and prepared to leave, feeling sad that this was probably the last time I would ever be in Dr. Flinn's presence again. But to my surprise, he stopped me at the door and asked if he could talk with me for a moment in the living room. Surprised, I followed him until he stopped in front of the beautiful hand-carved oak bookcase that covered the entire rear wall.

"I wanted to talk to you earlier but never got the chance," he said, still clutching the leather wine bag I had given him. He had been holding it tight all night. "I guess parties are not the best place for quiet conversations."

"I wanted to talk to you too, but you looked so busy hosting the party. I really enjoyed the class. I learned a lot from all the reading you assigned. And I enjoyed all the discussions we had. You managed to engage the entire class."

"You contributed a lot to those discussions. I always liked listening to your comments and reactions."

"Thank you," I replied, my heart pounding.

"I'll miss your class."

"I will too."

We stood there in silence, awkward as teenagers on a first date.

"Well, thanks again," I blurred out, turning toward the door.

"Wait," he said, stepping in front of me.

"I wanted to wait until the class was over, but I wonder if you might be interested in having dinner with me some night when you're free."

I was so startled, I couldn't immediately reply.

"But you're . . . you're married!"

"Married? Oh, no. I'm not married. I've been divorced for seven years now."

"But you have children, right?"

"Yes, I do. Eight, in fact. The youngest is now ten."

My legs were so wobbly I thought I would collapse.

"I have four sons and four daughters. Two of them are living here with me. I think you met my daughter, Carol, at the door."

"Yes, I did."

"I can understand if you are hesitant, considering the differences in our circumstances, but something inside me is telling me I need to do this."

"Actually," I stammered, "I would be honored to have dinner with you,"

"That's wonderful," he laughed. "That means our enjoyable conversations can continue. Since I already have your telephone number among my school papers, I shall give you a call this Friday evening and we can make arrangements then."

"Terrific," I replied, my heart thumping so fast and loud, I feared he might hear it.

We shook hands and I floated down the stairs like someone who had just grown wings.

When I got outside my father was waiting patiently in the old Rambler. He was smoking a cigarette and drinking coffee he had gotten from the Miss America Diner on Stegman Parkway.

"So how did it go?" he asked.

"Great. But I can't believe what happened. He asked me to dinner?'

Mick threw his cigarette out the window and faced me.

"I happened to be chatting with his landlord, an old biddy, and she said he was a character. A *real ladies man*. She told me she didn't trust him at all."

"Well, she certainly doesn't know him the way I do. He's one of the kindest and smartest people I ever met."

My father was silent for a moment staring into my eyes.

"Are you sure about that?"

"Yes. He's a wonderful man. I learned a lot from him this summer in class."

"Well, you're an adult now. You can probably figure things out for yourself. If you like the guy and think he's O.K., that's fine by me.'

"How do you think Mom will react?"

"You know your mother. She thinks you're still in kindergarten."

Wait until she finds out I have a date with a man who is divorced and has eight children, I thought. She'll either faint or tie me to the bed post. As understanding as my father was, I didn't want to mention the eight kids at that point.

"So when is this date you're going on?" he asked, starting up the Rambler and easing his way out of the parking spot.

"I don't know yet. He's going to call tomorrow and we'll plan something then."

"O.K. Just remember if you ever need my help, I'm always in your corner, Patsy."

I laughed. Mick always talked like some guy in the Mafia, but in reality he was as soft as a kitten. Years later I came to accept the idea that women marry men pretty much like their fathers. I was lucky that both my father and husband were gentle, caring men who wanted only to love and protect me.

But as I sat in the old Rambler that night I had no way of seeing into the future. What lay in store for me was a blank open notebook and I was the one to fill the pages.

That night's euphoria was quickly destroyed when I got back to the apartment and my mother began quizzing me.

"I hope you didn't do any drugs there," she said, sniffing my clothes for the scent of weed.

"No, I did not do drugs, Ma."

"I'm only asking because that professor of yours sounds like a hippy to me. You said he has long hair and a beard, right?"

"Yes, but that doesn't mean he takes drugs."

"Well, nowadays you never know. Young people are going crazy protesting at college campuses and marching on Washington in those funny clothes I would not be caught dead in."

"You mean bell bottoms and tie dye shirts?"

"I don't know what they're called but they look like things from inside a dumpster."

My poor mother was a victim of the times and circumstances. It was the early seventies and every night on T.V. there were scenes of long-haired kids carrying signs protesting the war, storming college buildings and demanding rights for women, gays, blacks, and other minorities. She pictured Greenwich Village as a place where everyone did drugs, lived in sin, and fornicated with strangers. She thought professors were communists and Archie Bunker a genius. When I finally got up the courage to tell her I was going on a date with my former professor, she nearly passed out.

"Are you crazy? She screamed so loudly I knew everyone in the tenement was now awake and listening. "This man is old enough to be your father. He's even old enough to go out with me."

My father, who enjoyed tormenting my mother whenever he got the chance, was quick to respond.

"He's a smart man, King Farouk. Why the hell would he want to go out with you?"

King Karouk was his nickname for my mother, a dictator who ruled with an iron fist and a loud mouth.

"All you men are alike," my mother said. "I don't trust any one of you. And I especially don't trust bearded beatniks."

I managed to slip away and into the quiet of my windowless bedroom. The layout of that flat left much to be desired. If we had "company" people would have to walk through the bedroom just to reach the living room. In short there was no privacy anywhere.

The next day when the phone rang about noon I rushed to pick it up, but my mother got there before me. I prayed it wasn't Doctor Flinn, but my prayers were not answered.

"Hello," my mother shouted into the receiver. "Who's there?"

I tried to grab the phone away, but she held on to it like a pit bull clamped onto a human leg.

"Oh, so you're my daughter's teacher? Well, I just want you to know . . ."

I grabbed the phone.

"Hello, Professor. Thank you for calling."

My mother was standing so close she was almost on top of me, trying to hear the conversation. I was so rattled, I could barely speak.

"Yes. . . yes. That was my mother. She's a little . . . little. . .deaf at times."

Fortunately, I heard him ask if Friday at 7 p.m. was a good time to meet.

"Fine. I'll see you then."

I hung up quickly before my mother had a chance to do any more damage.

"I bet you're going to Greenwich Village with that man. Am I right?"

"I don't know. We didn't get a chance to talk about that."

"Well, just make sure this so called restaurant is not in a hotel lobby." She stormed off into the kitchen banging a few old pots along the way.

When Friday rolled around, I made sure I was out of the apartment and waiting in front of the apartment for Dr. Flinn's arrival.

At seven sharp, a small yellow convertible whizzed around the corner of 4th and Adams Street and there in the front seat driving I saw my handsome professor. His hair was freshly cut and trimmed and there was a big smile on his face when he saw me standing there.

Some nosy neighbors were watching from the tenement across the street as he climbed out of the convertible and rushed to open the passenger door for me.

It wasn't until we were about to drive away that I saw my father heading toward us from the doorway of the Spot Tavern where he moonlighted as a bartender.

"Hi," he waved. "I just wanted to meet and say hello to the professor before you left."

Dr. Flinn got out of the car and shook my father's hand.

"My name's Gene. It's nice to meet you, Mr. Pean."

"Nice meeting you too, Gene. You guys have a good time tonight. Just drive carefully and be sure to take good care of my daughter, O.K."

"I will certainly do that, Mr. Pean."

"Call me Mick."

"Mick, I will do that."

I looked up and saw my mother gazing down at us from her window.

"Well, I guess we better be off now" I said, winking at my father.

"See you later, you two. I hope you have a very nice dinner."

CHAPTER SEVEN

Synchronicity and the Collective Unconscious

In every moment, the universe is whispering to us. Jung

MY MOTHER WAS right. We were on our way to Greenwich Village and I couldn't have been happier.

To me Greenwich Village meant bookshops, art galleries, cozy cafes, exotic shops that imported French cheese and artisan breads and restaurants that catered to every taste.

Our ride to the city was equally exciting. It was a beautiful summer night, pleasantly warm with a soft refreshing breeze that made the air clear and refreshing. With the top down on the ***yellow submarine,*** as Gene called his convertible Karma Ghia, we sailed along the narrow winding streets of Hoboken and through the Holland Tunnel to the Big Apple.

Gene seemed as excited and happy as I was and I remember we never stopped talking for a minute.

"Dr. Flinn. . . ." I began.

"I think it's about time you called me Gene," he laughed. "Our class is long over."

"O.K., Gene. By the way I really like that name."

"And I like your name Patricia," he said, glancing over at me. "Beautiful Patricia is what I shall you from now on. Or maybe Tricia. I like Tricia too."

When he saw that I had begun to blush, he laughed.

"Actually Eugene means well-born and Patricia also means well-born. Now isn't that a coincidence?"

We would later discover another strange coincidence in our lives. Both of us had the same nun for a teacher. Sister Catherine Eucaria had just entered the convent as a young woman of 18 when Gene was a first grade student in Our Lady of Victories grammar school in Jersey City.

She taught him how to make the number 4 on paper with a real pen. I later learned that Gene had skipped kindergarten and had gone right into first grade. Since no one had ever taught him to write numbers, he was a little frustrated and angry with himself that he couldn't master the technique while his classmate Albert Prongay was drawing so many 4s' they covered his entire sheet of paper. Sister Eucharia was not one for coddling.

"Hold the pen this way, Eugene, and practice, practice, practice."

Gene went home in tears telling his mother he was going to be left back in school for being a dummy because he couldn't draw a 4.

All night his mother, Agnes, practiced with him and eventually Gene got it. The next day in class he challenged Albert Prongay to a contest to see who could draw the fastest 4s. Gene won by a milestone.

Years later in 1967, Sister Eucharia became my Latin teacher at Sacred Heart Academy. She was an old woman by then and the years had been rough on her. The poor woman had skin cancer and had to wear plastic bags around her hands when she came to class.

Since we were all stupid teenagers and insensitive, we invented all kinds of wild tales to explain the plastic bags.

"She wants to conceal her fingerprints when the cops investigate the murder of our Mother Superior," I told my friends at lunch one day. When I got a laugh, I elaborated even more. "Or maybe she is getting ready to suffocate the next student who cannot translate correctly the first ten pages of Caesar's Gallic Wars."

Fortunately the nuns never learned of my outlandish stories or I would have been suspended for days. No one ever joked or laughed in Sister Eucharia's class. She was a strict taskmaster and if you were not prepared for the day's lesson, you were scolded and given twenty-five or more pages of the Gallic Wars to translate as punishment.

Driving through the Holland Tunnel on that our first date, Gene and I shared these memories of Sister Eucharia and were elated to learn we had so many things in common despite our age differences.

When we finally arrived in Greenwich Village, Gene parked the Yellow Submarine in a tight spot only a short distance away from the restaurant he had chosen.

He hopped out of the car and ran over to open my door. None of my previous boyfriends had ever done such a thing and I was highly amused but delighted. It was the height of the women's liberation movement which I firmly supported. Nevertheless, I was secretly thrilled to be treated in such an old-fashioned way. I felt like some elegant lady from a 1940s' classical movie starring Humphrey Bogart and Lauren Bacall.

I took Gene's hand as we crossed the street together and headed toward the *Paradox* café. It was a moment I will never forget-- the first time we were a couple holding hands together. Something that we were destined to do for the next forty-seven years.

The Paradox was certainly an off-beat restaurant, but typical of Greenwich Village in the 60s and 70s. My mother would have been unhappy I was there, but I was ecstatic. It was an introduction to a whole new world. We were dining under the stars and drinking wine in the moonlight. The Paradox had a big back yard with a long table that sat about 20 diners, all eating beside one another like family. There were several cats roaming under the table and hand-painted clay pots brimming with fresh flowers on every available shelf. Several overhead fans were swirling madly to keep the summer bugs away while people drank and enjoyed their meals.

"I hope you like this," Gene asked, watching my reaction. "I had the feeling you might enjoy something just a little different."

"I love it," I replied. "It's so cozy and friendly here. And I'm really impressed with the tables overflowing with free books for people to take home."

"Yes, that is a wonderful after-dinner treat. But wait until you read the menu. You'll be really surprised."

He was right. When a young woman with long blond braids, wearing a tie dye silk blouse with love beads greeted us, she handed us two menus the size of posters and told us to sit anywhere we liked.

Gene suggested we sit near the kitchen so we could sample all the delicious scents emanating from inside.

The specials of the day were seaweed sautéed in lemon butter mixed with dandelions and wild mushrooms, and a vegetarian dish of raw carrots, honeyed turnips and mashed avocado, garnished with basil and parsley and served in a large wooden bowl as round as an extra large pizza pie. Both dishes cost 75 cents.

"I hope you don't think I'm a cheapskate, but I sensed you would enjoy the crazy flavor of this place. I came here once before and it really brought back memories of the small French bistro I visited during the war that was run by a family of eccentrics who lived on vegetables grown in their backyard garden. They had a cat named Inky whom they adored since he ate all the mice that nightly crept into their home."

I learned then that Gene had fought in France during the Normandy invasion. It was a little strange to think my father had been fighting in Italy and North Africa at the same time. The only stories about the war my father ever mentioned was when he lost his rifle in a crap game and how he swallowed bugs the size of his fist when he tried to eat his army rations in his pup tent at night.

Gene told me he could have received a deferment because of an eye injury he had suffered as a teenager when he was deliberately shot with a staple by a neighborhood kid.

"When it was time for the eye test, I covered my bad eye and read the chart with my good eye. Fortunately, the doctor was not paying attention so I got away with it."

"It's remarkable you did something like that since a deferment could have saved you from fighting in the war," I said, genuinely impressed.

"I needed to do my share. Stopping Hitler was a lot different than dropping Napalm on innocent people in the Vietnamese War."

We were talking about so many things that I barely noticed my seaweed supper when it arrived. Food was not important. I was too overwhelmed with Gene's presence.

It was a wonderful feeling having him beside me, our arms touching, our faces only a few inches apart. I had never felt anything like that before. It was more than magnetic.

Later that night we went for a stroll along the lively, colorful streets, gazing up at the charming brownstones sporting overflowing flower pots in windows and front steps. The strong sweet scent of marijuana hung in the air as we passed shops selling everything from books to kitchen gadgets. We had no need of drugs to feel what we were beginning to experience that evening.

I knew Gene felt the same way I did from the way he looked at me and smiled. By the time we left the Village, rode back home and found ourselves in the hallway of my old tenement, I was hoping he would kiss me.

"Let's do this again," he smiled. "I had a great time tonight."

"I would love that," I whispered. I was afraid my mother would hear us from the apartment two flights up.

"Great. I'll plan another adventure that I think you might like. Call you tomorrow."

My energy was so high that night, I couldn't fall asleep but that didn't stop me from dreaming. I was flying across a snow covered mountain overlooking a cozy wind-swept village surrounded by sparkling blue lakes and tall lush green trees. In the distance muffled within a pillow of clouds came the sound of someone singing. As I got closer, I realized it was Gene, holding out his arms as he beckoned me forward.

CHAPTER EIGHT

The Force of Gravity on Mass in Motion

Life is strong and fragile. It's a paradox.
. . It's both things. Joan Jett

1 970 WAS A strange year. At the same time the war in Viet Nam was raging and disillusioned angry protesters were being dragged off to jail for rioting in the streets and shutting down college campuses, people were sitting in movie houses, crying their eyes out because Ali McGraw died of leukemia and left her young handsome husband, Ryan O'Neill alone to deal with his grief.

Love Story, based on the best-selling book by classic scholar and professor Eric Segal, had opened in theaters across the country. It later won several Oscars for its stars, McGraw and O'Neill.

When Gene heard about it, he purchased a copy of the book and left it in the hallway of my building. A few days later he was perplexed when he learned that I had never gotten it.

I had to explain that anything left in the hallway would probably be gone in a minute. Even mail addressed to Occupant was often stolen or misplaced. Surprised and amused, he promised he would buy me another copy.

Our next adventure was a trip to Alpine, New Jersey where we enjoyed a picnic in one of the highest and most scenic points in the state. We chose a spot beneath a towering old chestnut tree and spread a blanket for our lunch.

Gene bought a bottle of Sangria and some wine glasses, and I made the sandwiches.

My mother didn't complain too much when she heard we were going on a picnic. I suppose she thought that was a lot safer than some smoky joint in the Village.

Gene brought along Oscar Williams anthology to read some poems. He was a fan of e.e. cummings and he enjoyed reading *In Just Spring*. Every time he read the words "mud luscious" and "puddle wonderful," he laughed like a kid.

He also loved Robert Frost, especially *Stopping By Woods On a Snowy Evening*. *"My little horse must think it queer, to stop without a farmhouse near."*

The cadence of his voice reminded me of a cool waterfall in the forest. When he came to the line about *miles to go before I sleep,* he said the words with such feeling, I got goose bumps.

I chose Matthew Arnold's Dover Beach because I especially liked the stanza

> *Ah, love, let us be true to one another! For the world, which seems to lie before us like a land of dreams, so various, so beautiful, so new, Hath really neither joy, nor love, nor light, and we are here as on a darkening plain.*

Fortunately, we were not on a darkening plain on that gorgeous day in June 1970. We were sitting under a chestnut tree and savoring the delicious taste of poetry and soggy egg sandwiches on rye. The day was filled with glistening sunshine and dancing light, bathing every blade of grass and every leaf on every tree with a crystallized brilliance I had never seen before.

We chatted about everything under the sun, our spirits soaring. At one point, Gene jumped up from the blanket--, a half-eaten tomato falling on his dark blue turtleneck,--and grabbed hold of the chestnut tree behind us.

"You know what?" he said, his eyes alive with joy. "I'm going to make this day last forever by signing our names into the truck of this beautiful old tree which I'm sure will be here long after we are both gone."

With that, he took hold of his small pocket knife and began drawing a heart. Inside he wrote **Gene loves Tricia July 26, 1970.**

The next day we met again, this time in Lincoln Park Jersey City where we jogged together for the first time. Although it was a hot day, it was the easiest run I ever had since I was floating on cloud nine, overflowing with sheer happiness.

Later that afternoon Gene suggested we have lunch at the White Castle on Kennedy Boulevard near Journal Square.

"It's a tacky hamburger joint, as you probably know, but since it's built in the shape of a magical castle from mythology, I thought it might be fun."

On the way, Gene stopped in front of a small corner liquor store and bought a bottle of champagne.

"What's the celebration?" I asked, laughing. "Hamburgers and champagne."

"Us," he winked. "Life doesn't get any better than this."

After lunch, we drove around in the yellow submarine for about an hour and then Gene found a secluded spot in Lincoln Park alongside the lake.

"I wrote you a poem," he said. "Want to hear it?"

"Of course," I said, astonished I had inspired a poem, something I always imagined, but never thought possible.

"I called it **Alpine.** I got the idea after our visit on Sunday.

> *There, in our balcony, we stood*
> *You and I*
> *So far from the river*
> *So close to the sky*
> *Absorbed in a mystery*
> *Delicately spun, caressed by the*
> *Breeze, warmed by the sun.*
> *Warmed from the inside, as well as without*
> *By the flames of feeling what love is about.*
> *Two on a rampaging roll-a-coaster*

Just held in the sky by a railing
… and trust
But that was yesterday
And in the calm of today the mountains
Of Alpine seem far, far away.
Yet though yesterday's gone it lingers
Somehow
For the kisses we share are part of us now,
And I shall always remember
How we stood, you and I
So far from the river
So close to the sky.

We saw each other practically every day that summer. Gene would spin around the corner of Adams Street in his little yellow submarine, I would hop in, and we'd be off for brunch in a mountainside café, or a walk along the beach at Spring Lake, or we might ride through the Holland Tunnel and see a Broadway or off-Broadway play. Sometimes we would go to some *avant garde* movie house showing a Fellini film or take in a weird Happening in an east village loft.

One night Gene, who was reviewing plays for the Jersey Journal arts pages, managed to get tickets to **Jacque Brel is Alive and Well and Living in Paris.**

I was mesmerized by the songs and brilliant music of Brel, and I loved the small intimate setting of the charming Village Gate theater. We held hands during the entire production, and after the show Gene bought me the show's album.

I played that record so many times I learned every song by heart, and even some French lyrics too. I would sing as we rode along in the yellow submarine.

Sometimes after a show, we would wander through the village and stop for a quick snack and a drink in **Chumley's Pub** or visit the little piano bar we came to love, **Maria Crisis.**

Maria was the owner of the café, but she was the main attraction as a blue's singer and talented pianist. One night when I had the opportunity to speak with her, I told her she sounded like Billy Holiday.

"Thank you, Darling, but I ain't no Billy Holiday. She was the very best. Me? I'm just here playing around on my little old piano."

On a lovely Sunday in late July Gene and I took a trip to a Roosevelt Island nursing home where we met Dominick, a Catholic priest serving as a Chaplin there. He was a good friend of Gene's and I was more than happy to meet him. Unlike so many priests I had known from the past, he was young, handsome, and very much alive.

The first thing he did when he saw me was to open his arms wide, embrace me and give me a big kiss on my right cheek.

"Oh, Patricia, what a beautiful name! Just right for a beautiful girl like you. I am truly delighted to meet you."

He turned to Gene and winked.

"I envy you, my friend. You found a lovely woman here. Make sure you take good care of her.

Gene laughed and gave him a playful slap on the back.

"Remember your vows or I will personally contact the Pope and have you sent to Outer Mongolia."

It was a magical afternoon as we drove along in the Yellow Submarine across the winding lanes of the sea-scented coastline, watching the sparkling rays of sunlight dance atop the blue water.

We talked about everything from the deceptions of Richard Nixon and Spiro Agnew to whether there was any hope for a church that was increasingly irrelevant to people's lives.

I remember the three of us jammed together in a small space meant just for two.

I was wearing a dress and stockings that day and I had to laugh when I caught Father Dominick eyeing my legs every time I had to shift in my seat to allow Gene to operate the gear shift. It was the first time I realized priests were not gods; just human men with human appetites. For Dominick it was a harmless flirtation on a lovely summer afternoon we would all remember with fondness.

After Gene and I had been married for three years, we learned that Dominick had left the priesthood, married a woman he met on a trip to Ireland, and eventually settled in a little village in Roscommon where he raised sheep and mended the broken spirits of the locals by telling them the bawdy jokes and stories he had heard in the priesthood.

Besides being a witty man, Dominick proved to be a real asset in my complicated relationship with my mother. Although she still disapproved of my dating "an older, divorced man" she was impressed when I told her that we had spent the day with a Catholic priest who was taking care of old women in a nursing home.

"At least there was one day I didn't have to worry about you and that professor alone together," she said, pouring herself a cup of tea.

"With that priest watching over you, there probably wasn't any funny business going on."

"Yeah, Ma. You're right," I said. "Father Dominick was certainly watching over me."

CHAPTER NINE

Thoughts Become Reality

Everything is possible if you can imagine it. Neville Goddard

S UMMER WAS QUICKLY coming to an end, and our carefree, sun-filled days of riding under the open skies in the yellow convertible were ending. We didn't mind, however, since we enjoyed sitting close and cozy in the warm enclosed cocoon of the front seat.

In September we returned to school. Gene resumed teaching, and I began my studies again.. Although we were pretty busy that fall our new schedules still allowed us time to get together. On the weekends we spent whole days together.

On Saturday mornings when we felt like traveling far from the city, we took trips to rural Hunterdon, Somerset, and Sussex counties passing horse farms, old general stories, antique shops, and open fields where we watched white wooly sheep with short black legs grazing in the grass and fat lazy cows contentedly watching the world go by.

October that year was blessed with bright dazzling sunlight and cool breezes that slowly undressed the autumn trees, ushering early leaves to fall in a riotous dance of grace and color.

By mid-November, however, nights became cooler, and some days were rainy and overcast. It was a day like this when Gene and I decided to visit Tice's Farm in Old Bergen County.

It was apple season and everywhere one looked, shelves, boxes and baskets were overflowing with ripe delicious apples. The enticing scent of freshly squeezed apple cider and warm apple pie perfumed the air and made one swoon with pleasure.

As Gene was later to write in a story entitled **November Rain**, which he dedicated to me, Tice's Farm was the living embodiment of *Keats's season of mists and mellow fruitfulness where apples were bending the mossed cottage trees."*

Neither of us knew if it were the scent of apples or the magical mood of the day, but we sensed we had reached a moment in our relationship that couldn't be ignored.

When we returned to the yellow submarine with our treasure of apples and cider, we sat and listened to the softly falling rain playing a tap dance upon the canvas roof.

Gene reached for my hand, and told me he loved me. I rested my head on his shoulder and whispered I loved him too, and that I wanted to be with him forever.

We knew there would be huge obstacles and problems ahead for us. My mother and his family for one, and difficult situations we couldn't even anticipate, but the only thing that seemed real was being there together at that moment in time.

We got engaged on Christmas Eve 1970. On our way to pick up the ring in Union, the yellow submarine got a flat tire and we had to stop in a gas station on Route 22 to have it fixed.

When I mentioned to the mechanic, a friendly older man with kind eyes and a day-old scratchy beard that we had just gotten engaged, he smiled, shook our hands, and reached for a bottle of Jamison Irish Whiskey from beneath a nearby counter.

"Here's to a long and happy marriage," he said, taking a big gulp and wiping his lips with the tail end of his dirty blue work shirt. "May you always remain in love."

We couldn't have asked for a better blessing. Although I was not used to drinking whiskey on an empty stomach, and I felt the burn for a good long time that morning, I never forgot the warmth and good will of that hard-working mechanic in that cluttered greasy gas station on Route 22 somewhere between Mountainside and Springfield, New Jersey.

CHAPTER TEN

When Anti-Particles Collide
With Light Photons

I just want to think like God thinks. Albert Einstein

WE ALSO NEVER forgot what happened that night at the midnight mass in the Catholic Church in Edgewater, not far from the home of the couple Gene had recently befriended.

Mary and Dave O'Hara had invited us for dinner to celebrate Christmas and our engagement. They had a lovely home and it was their suggestion we attend Midnight mass at St Michael's Church.

After a few Bloody Marys we were open to a new adventure, and since it had started to snow and looked very much like an old-fashioned Christmas in the country, we were excited to take the short drive through the scenic local neighborhood all aglow with bright colorful lights and festive decorations.

The church was packed with people all dressed in their holiday best, and the priest and altar boys, in their white and black cassocks, were marching up and down the aisles, blessing people, while the choir belted out a medley of traditional hymns and Christmas prayers.

Mary, Dave, Gene and I squeezed into a pew at the rear of the church and watched the joyful scene. The bloody Marys had warmed our hearts and stomachs and a peaceful bliss seemed to descend from the heavens, or at least from the choir loft, as music filled the church and people bowed their heads in prayer.

Everything was going fine, just the way you would expect a midnight mass to unfold in a Bing Crosby movie with everyone being charming and loving, while behind the stain-glass windows snow was falling in big buckets, coating the sidewalks and lawns with white magic.

When the service reached communion time, people folded their hands skyward, bowed their heads, and slowly made their way up the aisles to the main altar to receive the wafer and sip the blessed wine. We watched like curious pagan spectators as the rituals continued. But then something unexpected happened.

Perhaps she had consumed more than her share of the holy wine, or maybe she had drunk too many eggnogs spiked with rum at home, but at any rate an elderly woman sitting in a pew directly behind us began to sing off-key in a loud drunken voice.

People sitting near her tried their best to quiet her with loud "sssssssshhhhh," but this only seemed to encourage her, and she began not only to sing louder, but to begin a little dance in the pew, bumping against a very large woman in a long fur coat and wide fur hat.

At the altar the priest read from an oversized gold-embossed book. "And the lord said to his people. . ."

"Ba, Ba, Ba," the drunken lady yelled.

Gene and I began to laugh, but Mary and Dave looked at us as if we had just uttered an obscenity into the baby Jesus's ear.

Out of the corner of my eye, I saw two burly men in dark suits with carnations in their buttonholes come racing down the aisle toward the woman.

They elbowed their way into the small pew like two linebackers, knocking over the lady in the fur coat while grabbing hold of the singing, babbling woman.

They thrust their hands under her armpits and lifted her into the air like a little ragdoll. Then they dragged her from the pew, down the center aisle.

Another man, waiting at the exit, opened the door, and the two linebackers flung the woman down the steps into a deep pile of snow.

Although most people in the church were watching this drama and not what was happening on the altar, the priest and altar boys continued on with their robotic motions without blinking an eye.

We looked at each other in astonishment as the priest chanted, "Holy, holy, holy is the name of God in the highest. . ."

"Let's get out of here," Gene said, grabbing hold of my hand." I think we have seen enough of this place."

Mary and Dave watched us, shaking their heads.

"Hey, where are you going?' Dave said to Gene. "The mass is not over yet. You're creating a scene."

"I'm creating a scene?" Gene laughed. "What about those two bouncers for Jesus? Wasn't that quite a scene?"

Dave shrugged. "She was drunk."

"Perhaps but she didn't deserve that kind of treatment."

"Whatever," Dave replied, turning away. "Have a good holiday."

Outside we looked around, but the drunken lady was nowhere in sight. Gene said he hoped she had wandered off to the nearest bar to warm up."

"How about we do the same, Tricia?"

We never made it to the bar and we did not return to Mary and Dave's house either. We just sat in the heated comfort of the yellow submarine watching the snow fall in big fluffy flakes all around us.

In the weeks that followed I did a lot of thinking about religion, God, and life. Although I went to a Catholic grammar and high school, I never really believed in the church's teachings. So many of them struck me as absurd and downright silly. The idea of a God who lived way up in the sky and was always watching people sounded more like a peeping tom than a deity. The nuns and priests insisted God was love, but they warned he could send you to hell in a heartbeat if you broke any of his ten commandments. The story about babies going to purgatory if they weren't baptized also seemed mean and unfair to me. I tried to picture purgatory in my mind's eye but all I could imagine was a smelly place hanging in mid air like a stalled elevator stuck between floors. Even the idea that Jesus was sent by God, his own father, to die a horrible grisly death on the cross for my sins seemed totally unbelievable to me. Even at the age of ten I couldn't believe any loving father would do such a thing. Nor could I think of any sin I had committed that would have demanded such punishment.

But like most kids growing up in the fifties, I kept these questions to myself. Years later it was a joy and comfort when I was able to talk to Gene so freely and directly about my ideas.

I was intrigued the night Gene told me he believed that all things were composed of Divine energy, or the consciousness of God giving life and substance to all creation. This idea was so foreign to me I couldn't conceive of it.

"God is not outside us," he explained. "God is part of us. Think of a wave within the ocean. Every part of the ocean is in a wave, but the wave itself is unique as it rears its head for a short time from the depths. Once it crashes into the sandy shore, however, it returns effortlessly to the ocean."

"But if we have God within us, why is there so much evil and suffering in the world," I persisted. "It just doesn't make any sense"

"Because the vast majority of the human race has not awakened to this spiritual truth. They believe the old ideas we were taught as children that God was separate from them and always sitting in judgment of them. It's a belief based on fear rather than love."

"This was the God in the Old Testament."

"Yes, the kind of God primitive people could understand. This idea of God kept these people from their barbarous behaviors and tribal wars."

"But that is the God people today accept too."

"Yes, and unfortunately, that is what prevents their spiritual growth. Believing they are sinners separate from God they remain locked in a very low level of consciousness. They see and think from a dark space of fear and anger. They feel they are alone in this vast universe. Survival is a constant struggle. They cannot imagine their own connection with God or the spiritual powers bestowed on them."

"So what do you think happens to these people?

"I like to believe the story of the Prodigal Son. He wandered around in darkness for a long while, spending and wasting his fortune but eventually he woke up and returned home. He found to his surprise his father didn't judge him and never stopped loving him. He gave him back everything he had squandered."

"But if I remember correctly his brother resented that. He thought he was more deserving of his father's love since he stayed home and worked hard while his worthless brother was having a great time drinking, gambling and fornicating."

"He didn't understand unconditional love which is understandable from the human perspective. But the point of the story, I think, is that we must learn to see from the divine perspective."

"That's pretty hard to do."

"Not when people's consciousness begins to change, I think. Some people wake up slowly like a rose opening its petal in early spring. They sense there is more to life than just the outer reality they see all around them."

"Realists believe these people are dreamers, right?'

"Right. And thank heaven for dreamers. They move mankind forward. Today scientists are discovering more about the laws of this world and those of the subatomic world. Slowly they are learning what mystics knew for centuries and that is everything in the universe is connected and sustained by the same force called energy. In short, we are all one."

Perhaps my own consciousness had begun to change that night after talking to Gene, since I began to see him in another light. He was more than just a very smart and kind man. He was *divine* too.

CHAPTER ELEVEN

From Quarks to Quacks

Chaos when left alone tends to multiply. Stephen Hawkings

WHEN I ARRIVED home at 3 A.M. on that Christmas Eve night, I took off my new engagement ring and hid it in my pocketbook. I knew my mother would be waiting up for me, and ready to check if any buttons were missing from my winter coat. This was her way of knowing if any "necking" or "hanky-panky" had taken place.

As I suspected she was sitting at the kitchen table, bleary-eyed and annoyed.

"Do you know what time it is, young lady?"

"We were at Midnight Mass, Mom. Naturally, it's late."

"Midnight Mass does not go on until 3 in the morning. Where were you? I was worried sick."

"We celebrated at a friend's house."

"When I saw the snow falling, I thought you had an accident. I pictured you dead on the highway."

"I'm fine, just tired. I'm going to bed now. Good night."

"Not so fast. Come here and let me have a look at you."

Reluctantly, I approached her.

"You're missing another button."

"They don't sew them on very good these days."

"Buttons will stay on until someone pulls them off," she said, inching closer to smell my breath to see if I had been drinking."

"We stopped for hot chocolates on the way home, Ma."

"And what else did you have?"

"We had a lovely dinner at a friend's home."

I didn't want to mention the Bloody Marys.

"You were never out this late before."

"It's Christmas Eve. Or should I say it's now Christmas Day. Merry Christmas, Ma. I will talk to you in the morning."

I gave her a quick kiss on her cheek and hurried toward the bedroom.

But I made terrible mistake in my haste. I left my pocketbook on the kitchen table, and that *"was the knock on the door to my undoing."*

As I was about to fall asleep, my mother came charging like a bull into the room and flung herself down on the bed.

"What is this?" she asked holding up the ring.

"A ring," I said, trying my best to sound casual.

"And where did you get it?"

"Gene gave it to me."

"This looks like an engagement ring. Are you engaged? Are you crazy?"

"Which question should I answer?"

"Is that what you were doing tonight? Getting engaged to a man who is old enough to be your father?"

"Can we talk about this in the morning. I'm very tired now."

"Are you pregnant?"

"No, I am not pregnant and try to lower your voice. You will wake up the whole neighborhood."

"If you're not pregnant why get married?"

"Because I want to be with Gene. I love him."

Just then my father wandered into the room, looking punch drunk in his grey boxer shorts and Italian undershirt.

"What the hell is going on, King Farouk? Your voice could wake up the dead. I know it woke me up."

"Your daughter is engaged to be married to that hippy professor. Look. He gave her an engagement ring."

She tossed the ring to Mick who caught it with one hand.

"Wow, I bet he paid a pretty good bundle for this. Look at the size of this diamond."

Actually it was a small diamond, but since my father had never seen a diamond close-up before, he assumed it had to be expensive.

"Did you hear what I said?" my mother repeated "Your only daughter is engaged to be married to a man she met a few months ago."

"Well, she is nineteen now going on twenty. She's not a baby anymore, and if she is determined to be married, you can't stop her. She's smart enough to make her own life decisions now."

I could have kissed my father right there, but he looked too sleepy for a big embrace, so I just smiled at him and he smiled back.

"No wonder she is the way she is with you for a father."

She began walking around in circles, swinging her arms and pointing to my ring.

"She'll be sorry. Just you wait and see. Then she'll come running back and . . ."

Mick handed me back the ring.

"Go to bed, sweetheart. And don't fret. Everything will work out just fine."

I left for bed, but I never fell asleep that night. Despite my father's reassurances, I was terrified that things would only continue to get more chaotic. Gene and I would have to be pretty strong to withstand all the pressure.

My mother still didn't know Gene had eight kids, and I simply could not face her reaction when the time came to tell her. Also, I had no idea how Gene's children would react either when they heard the news their father wanted to get married again. I didn't know them at all since they lived with their mother in another state. There were so many pieces of the puzzle to fit together and obstacles to face in the days ahead, but the one thing I was certain about was that I wanted Gene in my life.

We decided that the wedding would take place June 5, 1971.

Gene's first marriage was in early February, a cold day with rain, wind, and snow. He told me that he should have listened to his heart because he did not want to go through with the marriage.

But everything had been rushed and arranged and his best man who happened to be his best and longest friend, told Gene almost everyone had misgivings on their wedding day.

Gene knew it was more than that, but he could think of no way to stop the ceremony. All the pews in the church were filled with family and friends and the reception had been planned and relatives were still arriving from far-flung places. How could he possibly stop the speeding train he was on?

Gene told me that story many times over the coming years and I think he did so to prove to me that he had absolutely no misgivings or anxious feelings about marrying me.

In fact, he wanted it to take place as soon as possible so we could spend years together and not waste any precious time dealing with people intent on separating us.

I felt the same way, but I was still in college and I wanted to graduate and then go to graduate school.

"I'll help you every step of the way," he promised. In fact. I think you should study for a Ph.D . That way there will be not one but two Dr. Flinns in the family."

In the early seventies there were still plenty of men who were threatened if their wives got academic degrees or held important jobs, but Gene was different. He was totally supportive and helpful in every way possible. I knew even then he wanted only the best for me.

If my mother could have accepted that truth, life would have been a whole lot easier for the both of us.

CHAPTER TWELVE

Radioactive Interactions across Time and Space

I like to think order exists somewhere, even if it shatters near me. Elizabeth Moon

ALTHOUGH I KNEW it would be a shocking announcement for everyone in our families, Gene and I decided to marry that coming June. We laughed at the conventional idea of a June wedding, but we knew it was the best time because the weather would be good, school would be over and we would be able to vacation together that summer.

One afternoon Gene and I decided to talk over our plans while going for a bike ride in Central Park. As we approached the corner of West 76th street, we saw a sign announcing that the Unitarian Church directly across from us was holding a poetry reading that evening.

"A church that appreciates poetry," Gene said. "Sounds pretty good to me. Want to check it out?"

Reverend Kellerman was the man in charge and what a stroke of luck that was! Unlike so many of the Catholic priests we had known, Reverend Kellerman was relaxed, warm and friendly. He was in his office when we arrived unannounced at his door.

"Come in," he said with a smile. "What can I do for you folks?"

"Well," Gene said, glancing at me. "We want to be married."

"Right now," he laughed.

"Well, maybe not this minute, but pretty soon. How about a day this June?"

"Well, that sounds fine with me, but I have to check my calendar. If there is an opening, we'll make it happen."

The three of us got along great that afternoon. We confided in him like old friends about our difficulties conforming to the rules and man-made dogmas of many churches and how refreshing it was to find a church so welcoming and accommodating.

"The Unitarians believe in uniting people not dividing them," he said, leaning back in his chair. "We welcome people who are seeking a more personal connection with spirit. And we love performing wedding ceremonies. What can be more personal then that?"

Over the next several weeks we read a great deal about the Unitarian Church. Its philosophy of respect for all creation and its community and social activism appealed to us.

Unlike the Catholic church we were not forced into making pledges that we would attend weekly mass, raise children as Catholics, or avoid birth control at all costs. Nor did we have to renounce other religions, or pray for those poor souls in purgatory who were never baptized.

We were more than delighted when Revered Kellerman called and said June 5th, a Saturday was open and available for our wedding. Starting time would be 11:30 a.m. and he would be the officiating minister. He assured us we could write our own vows and read anything from literature we liked.

"Although I really don't know you guys very well, I sense you are both on the same wavelength and that bodes well for a long and happy marriage," he said.

The only caution he offered was for our friends not to throw rice outside the church after the wedding.

"Steps covered in rice can get pretty slippery and we don't want people falling and breaking their necks on your big day.'

We assured him there would be no rice on June 5th. Just lots of kisses and hugs.

The next few months were stressful. There was one crisis after another with family members involving my mother, Gene's children, his ex-wife, and our friends.

Even some close friends told us we were making a big mistake getting married, but we did our best to ignore the negativity and listen to our hearts.

Gene's old buddies said marrying a younger woman would make him a laughing stock and probably a cuckold one day.

My friends tried to convince me that Gene could not be trusted because he was a divorced man.

Gene told me that some of his colleagues were gossiping behind his back too, especially the older women professors who enjoyed calling him the Playboy of the Western World, even before they knew we were engaged.

It's hard to imagine today the scandal that took place back then when a person got a divorce and dared to think about marrying someone else again. Today it is commonplace, but in the 60s' and 70s it was shocking to many people. As Henrik Ibsen once wrote at the end of his play Hedda Gabbler, a drama about an unhappy woman who left her husband, *"people just don't do those things."*

This was certainly the philosophy of Sister Madeline, a Catholic nun and a friend of my mother's for many years. One day when I returned from the library I learned that Sister Madeline was visiting and wanted to speak with me.

Sister Madeline was not your typical nun. In fact, there was little that was nun-like about her. She was loud, aggressive, and built like a longshoreman. Her face was square like her habit, and fiery-red.

She wore thick glasses as large as swim goggles and she had a mustache that she tried to hide by rubbing Noxima cream in thick slabs across her fat upper lip. Her front teeth were miles apart and when she occasionally smiled it looked like several teeth were missing. People tried not to stand too close when she spoke since showers of saliva flew from her mouth like spray from Niagara Falls.

She had worked in the Catholic orphanage where my grandmother was a cook and over the years she had managed to somehow promote herself to a more comfortable and profitable position in the convent and community by some magic and trickery that I could never understand.

Although she took a vow of poverty when she first entered the convent, she eventually owned a brand new car, shopped like a shopaholic, ate in expensive restaurants and traveled to Europe on yearly trips she herself never paid for.

Her biggest claim to fame was being mentioned in Frank Sinatra's biography on page 349. She carried the book everywhere and underlined the paragraph in red in case readers' eyes were poor.

> *Sister Madeline, of Our Lady of Grace Roman Catholic Church in Hoboken, New Jersey, so impressed Frank Sinatra with her unselfish devotion to people of his old townhome that he rewarded her with a brand new 1970 Chevy Station wagon and a one thousand dollar check which she could give to a charity of her choice.*

It didn't take a genius to know which charity she chose, but somehow even though she was as fake as a Ralph Lauren leather handbag made in China she managed to convince my mother that she could "put some sense into my head about marrying a divorced man."

At first Sister Madeline greeted me with a smile and asked me to sit down so we could have a nice little chat over tea.

"So, your mother tells me she is very upset since you are considering marrying your former professor."

"Yes, I am engaged to be married."

"And what about your former intention of becoming a nun?"

"Sister, when I was ten years old I imagined that for a short while, but I changed my mind when I entered fourth grade."

"Tell me, have you lost your faith?"

"No, I wouldn't say that. I have strong faith in a personal God. I just don't consider myself a Catholic anymore."

"Is that why you are considering marrying a man who is divorced and ex-communicated from the Catholic Church?"

"No. That has nothing to do with it. I'm marrying Gene because I love him."

"And does this man have any children?"

I couldn't lie, but I knew my mother was listening nearby and that this would be the first time she heard that Gene had eight children.

"Yes, he does have children," I whispered.

My mother dropped a tea cup into the sink and it shattered into little pieces.

"How many?"

"How many?"

"Yes, how many children does he have?"

"What difference does that make?" I asked.

"It makes a great deal of difference. How many children does this man have?"

"Eight. He had eight children, *according to my last count.*"

I said that last part as a joke naturally, hoping to lighten things up, but it didn't work. In fact, it backfired.

My mother gasped and grabbed her chest, shattering more cups as she staggered about the kitchen.

"I. . . I need to sit down," she groaned. "I think I am having a heart attack."

"Helen. Please remain calm. I'm in charge here."

Sister Madeline turned back to me.

"See now what you have done. You're poor mother who gave birth to you is suffering. You are literally killing her. Do you hear me? You are killing her. If she drops dead right here in this kitchen in front of us, you will be the one responsible."

"Sister, I think you should leave now. Things are getting out of control here."

I tried to get up, but Sister Madeline literally tackled me and shoved me back down.

"You are not going to marry this man and lose your eternal soul. I won't allow that."

"Sister, there is nothing you can do to change my decision."

"Oh no," she spat. "That's what you think. I have the power and the authority to have your mental state evaluated in a psychiatric institution. You are obviously crazy to even think of marriage at your age."

"What do you know about marriage?" I asked, my temper beginning to flare.

"You're a nun. You know nothing about marriage."

"I know that marrying a man who is divorced is a mortal sin. You will be excommunicated by the church and your soul will be in grave danger."

"What the hell is going on here," my father said, storming into the apartment with a large bottle of red wine in his hands. "I could hear shouting a mile away."

"Your daughter is about to marry a man with eight children," my mother cried, still clutching her chest. "Could things get any worse?"

"Yes. I think I heard this nun say she was thinking of sending our daughter to a mental hospital. Now if that is true I want this woman out of our house immediately. She has no right to talk to Patsy like that."

"I was simply warning your daughter she is in danger of making a grave mistake. It is obvious her brain has been twisted by this man and she does not know what she is doing."

"You know nothing about my daughter or her feelings so please leave now, Sister, and do not interfere in our lives again."

Sister Madeline knew he meant business, so with her long black veils swinging into motion, she rose from her chair and headed for the door.

"Oh, no wonder our daughter is the way she is with you for a father," my mother swore, flinging herself onto the living room couch that had seen better days. "You should be ashamed of yourself treating a holy nun like that."

"*Holy?* You can't be serious, King Farouk. The only thing *holy* about that woman are the *holes* in her stockings."

He winked at me and then proceeded to the kitchen in search of a bottle opener. The next day Gene could not believe what had happened when I told him about Sister Madeline. He was very angry at first, but soon we were laughing.

"Life is a jest and all things show it. I thought so once and now I know it."

"Where did that come from?" I asked.

"From John Gay's headstone.," Gene replied. "He was a smart man with a wonderful sense of humor. He realized life was absurd at times and just laughed at it. It was his way of surviving in this crazy world."

CHAPTER THIRTEEN

The X-Factor

Chance favors the prepared mind. Louis Pasteur

A S OUR WEDDING day approached, things got even crazier. Since I didn't have a job I had no income. Therefore I could not buy my own wedding dress, and it was obvious I could not ask my mother to help since she had informed me she would not be attending the wedding ceremony.

I also didn't have the heart to ask my father since I knew he would probably have to borrow the money from the loan sharks and I certainly did not want him to do that. I was content to just wear a nice dress and forget about a traditional gown.

When Gene eventually learned what was going on, he was tactful but determined.

"It's really no problem, Tricia. I will buy your wedding dress. It's the least I can do since you wouldn't need one if I didn't ask you to marry me, right?'

That seemed like funny logic to me, but it was just like Gene. Totally caring and unselfish.

My dress was simple but lovely. It had a high neck collar with pretty lace across the bust and long puffy sleeves that were both casual and elegant. Its soft cotton fabric flowed gracefully from my waist to my feet and felt wonderfully cool and comfortable against my legs. A pale blue ribbon around the waist added a splash of color and verve to the overall design.

Several years after we were married, Gene wrote a three-act play entitled *"And Now the Groom Dances with the Photographer."*

It was a satire on commercialized wedding receptions. When we staged it at Rutgers University, we converted the performance space into a large room that was designed to look like a reception hall where a wedding was about to take place. The play poked fun at all the celebratory rituals: the staged photos of the bride and groom; the blaring music performed by tone-deaf musicians; the harried waiters rushing around carrying trays of burned beef and overcooked chicken, and on and on.

We certainly did not want this kind of reception. Instead, after much thought, we decided to rent a family home down the Jersey Shore.

We envisioned a quiet place where we would enjoy a peaceful, blissful honeymoon.

So one day in April when the first hints of spring were in the air, we drove south to look for rental properties. People were already beginning to book their summer vacations, so we needed to act fast if we wanted something good on the water.

We stopped in a small real estate office in Brick Town, but there was only one man there and he was talking on the phone. When he saw us, he began gesturing for us to sit.

He was wearing a black shiny suit, a diamond pinkie ring, and a watch the size of a dinner plate.

"You're crazy if you pass this one up," he said into the phone. "I'm telling you, take my advice, and invest your money now."

Gene and I took one look around the office that was cluttered with mail and three-year old magazines.

"I think we should leave," Gene whispered.

We walked toward the door, but suddenly the man on the phone jumped up and ran toward us.

"Hey, wait. Where are you folks going? I'll be with you in a minute."

"Thanks," Gene said. "But we must be off now. Money is burning a big hole in my pocket and so I have to invest it immediately."

On the way out, I began laughing and grabbed a paper that listed nearby rentals. We decided to go to lunch and scan the rentals at our leisure.

We discovered a colorful bistro only two blocks away and sat down to tea and tuna fish sandwiches. Ever since we began eating together, Gene noticed my habit of putting ketchup on tuna fish and once he tried it, he liked it so much he began doing the same thing every time we ordered tuna.

"Someday maybe fifty years from now, we'll be like those old married couples who look alike and do so many things together, they become twins," I said. "Would you like that, Gene?"

"Why wait fifty years? He laughed. "Let's be twins now."

We scanned the listings while we ate, and Gene checked off a few promising ones with his red grading pen.

"This one sounds nice. *Two bedrooms private home on the Metedeconk River: Large kitchen, living and dining room and two full bathrooms. Four hundred dollars a week.* Not bad. What do you think?"

Sounds great but why would we need two bedrooms?" I teased. "You're not trying to tell me something, are you, Gene?"

"No silly. I'm thinking we may need another bed if your father wants to visit."

"You are so thoughtful, Gene. There aren't many men in this world who would want their father-in-law around on their honeymoon."

"You're father is a very special man, Trish. I like him very much. After all, he gave me you."

We kissed across the table, smearing ketchup on each other's lips.

"Besides I know your father has hit it off with my friend Paul. I think they might both enjoy going to the race track. Monmouth Raceway is only a short drive away. One day, they can visit us and we'll all go to the racetrack together."

"That will be fun. My father will be in heaven. There is nothing he likes more than spending a day away from my mother for a visit with horses."

"Mick sounds like Swift's Gulliver. Maybe that's why I like him so much."

We were in luck. The first house we looked at was just about perfect. The back patio faced the River and we could dive right into the water or go rowing in the cool mornings or late afternoon once the heat had gone down.

A woman answered the phone when we called to inquire.

She was very friendly and invited us to come right over. She was waiting at the front door when we arrived She was a short, plump woman of fifty with streaks of grey in her clipped sandy hair.

We made our introductions and enjoyed a bit of small talk about the weather, while wiping our shoes on the mat that read "Home Sweet Home."

"So glad I answered the telly," she smiled, leading us into her living room. "Sometimes I don't answer it since one of my friends talks my ears off and it's hard to end the conversation without being rude."

"Are you English?" Gene asked. "I detect an accent."

"Yes, I am. Are you familiar with the Lake district?"

"Of course. The home of many of our best English authors, Wordsworth, Shelley, Coleridge . . ."

"And you must be an English professor."

"That I am."

"See, we're both psychic," she said laughing.

We were not sure whether we should mention that we wanted to hold a wedding reception in her house. We did not want to be dishonest, but we knew our chances of renting a house were slim if we revealed that immediately.

Besides we also wanted the home as our private honeymoon cottage and if anything went amiss at the reception we would have a whole week to clean things up and repair any damage.

Mrs. Trumley talked a bit about her family in Dorset while she gave us a tour of the house. It was so cozy and clean we felt instantly at home. Each room had a lovely Tiffany lamp either hanging from the ceiling or resting atop a table or desk.

There was plenty of natural light flooding each room. Sliding glass doors in the kitchen led onto a comfortable patio with its river view and dock area. In the center of the room was a lovely round oak table upon which a colorful bowl filled with fresh fruit and flowers lent a lovely scent and character to the space.

There were two bedrooms about the same size that were filled with sunlight streaming through large windows and skylights. Our favorite room was the library that contained several comfortable reclining chairs and a large black leather sofa that sat directly in front of a tall teakwood bookshelf. Five more tiffany lamps provided warm splashes of color and soft light to the tranquil décor. It was the ideal space to while away a rainy afternoon with a fascinating book and a hot cup of tea.

Gene enjoyed his brandy in those days and I could imagine him sitting there on that leather sofa with a tumbler of **Courvoisier** in his hand and his writing pad on his lap.

Mrs. Trumley, unlike most British people, was not at all reserved or snobbishly proper. She revealed so much about herself that afternoon that we felt we had known her for years.

She confessed that her husband had died only a year ago and that she had no children, but kept herself busy volunteering at the community food bank and acting in plays in the local theater.

When Gene heard this, his ears perked up.

"Our dream is to own a theater someday and see our plays performed. We like to act and direct. Trisha is quite the actress."

Mrs. Trumley smiled at me and asked what roles I had played.

When I told her I was Linda Loman in Arthur Miller's The Death of a Salesman, she seemed impressed.

"Maybe it's because I am British and my accent strikes people as funny, but it seems all the roles I get are comedic. I would love to sink my teeth into a nice juicy drama, but alas, I play characters like Mama in **You Can't Take It With You.**"

"That a great role," I said. "That play is a classic and Mama is one of the leads."

I think that made her feel better.

"Yes," Gene continued. "Mama was the artist in that eccentric family. She was always carrying around a typewriter determined to compose her masterpiece. She was a wonderful character and I'm sure you did a great job bringing her to life on stage."

"Thank you," Mrs. Trumley replied, delighted by the unexpected compliment. She was so caught up in our conversation, she barely asked us any questions about why we wanted to rent her house.

At one point she even invited us for tea and biscuits in her charming kitchen. That gave us a chance to sit down and enjoy the feeling of what it would be like to live there for a few days.

Mrs. Trumley continued to chat away, even quoting a few lines from Wordsworth, her favorite poem.

"The child is father of the man, trailing clouds of glory do we come . . . ."

Gene and I were still wondering if we should tell Mrs. Trumley about the wedding when suddenly she turned to us and asked, "So when are you two planning on getting married? Do you have a date yet?"

We were startled.

"Oh, don't be surprised," she laughed. "I'm a bit psychic. Really I am. My grandmother taught me how to meditate and sense things when I was a little girl. I've been practicing ever since then, but I'm also a good observer of people and I can tell you two are very much in love. Most people who are married have lost that glow, unfortunately."

She placed two delicate china cups and saucers on a tray and sat down across from us.

"We're getting married on June 5th," Gene confessed. "And we were hoping to have a small gathering in a house we would rent here at the shore."

"Like my house?"

"Yes. We were hoping to rent your home on June 4th until June 18th."

"Well," Mrs Trumley said after a short pause. "Those two weeks are still available, but you must promise me that you will take good care of my home and treat it like your own."

"That's a promise," Gene replied.

"Very good then. "You just need to sign a few papers confirming our agreement on dates and price. For now, however, let's enjoy our tea and theater chat.

CHAPTER FOURTEEN

String Theory and the Law of Entanglement

We are not separated parts of a whole but rather we are the Whole. Barbara Brennan

MANY COUPLES ARE happy getting involved in all the elaborate preparations and pre-marital rituals that have been handed down from one generation to another when a wedding is in sight. These include the bridal shower, the bachelor party, the endless consultations with bridesmaids and relatives, the honeymoon arrangements, and the careful hiring of photographers and chauffeurs, to name just a few.

Gene and I didn't need or want any of these things, but the days leading up to June 5th were still chaotic and stressful.

Some days blazed by, while others poked along like an old man on his last legs. Years later when I was introduced to Quantum mechanics, I understood first hand what Einstein's theory of relativity was all about. When asked to explain it, Einstein said "when a man is with a pretty woman time goes very fast. When a person is waiting for her doctor to call, time takes forever."

My mother was doing everything she could to prevent our marriage and so she really went crazy when she learned my father would not only attend the ceremony but be an active part of it. He agreed and was more than happy when I asked him to walk me down the aisle of the Unitarian Church.

Fortunately, Mick learned after years of living with my mother how to tune her out when her nagging became too much to bear. He would turn up the volume on the radio and listen to his favorite opera while relaxing with a few glasses of red wine.

"Pay no attention to King Farouk," he would tell me. "She is having just another one of her schizophrenia attacks. When she can't get her way this is what happens. But she'll calm down eventually and see what a nice guy Gene is."

I tried talking to my mother and did my best to understand her concern for me. But she refused to listen to anything I had to say. She was determined to change my mind about Gene and I simply would not let that happen.

Sadly, my poor father bore the brunt of my mother's tirades since I was out of the house most of the time. He was definitely in my corner during those days and all the days that followed in the weeks and years ahead after Gene and I were married.

When June 5th 1971 did finally arrive, it was a magical day in every sense of the word. The sky was the deepest blue I had ever seen filled with massive white cumulus clouds floating in a sea of blue-velvet. The comfortable temperature (low 70's) was perfect with a gentle breeze and no humidity on an early June day.

That morning as I dressed for my wedding, my mother made one last desperate attempt to stop me. She sat in the kitchen clutching a pair of rosary beads praying that I would come to my senses.

Meanwhile in another room my father was already dressed in his tux. It was the first time he had ever worn a tux and I was relieved he managed to figure out how to put on a bow tie and cummerbund.

It was ten o'clock when we finally left the apartment, praying that the Holland Tunnel would not be jammed with weekend traffic.

Thankfully, there were few cars on the road and so we made it to the church in plenty of time. Central Park was packed with people on such a beautiful day. Some were jogging, some cycling, some walking their dogs, or roller-skating. There were even a few cops riding their horses along the leafy pathways. After my father found a parking space, we got out and walked a few short blocks to the church.

"Oh, look at the bride," a little girl shouted. "She's getting married today, Mommy."

"You'll be sorry," a boy on a bike shouted as he rode by.

"Good luck, honey," an elderly woman walking with a cane said as we passed her.

As we climbed the steps of the church, I spotted Gene pacing up and down in the front of the altar. He looked so handsome in his white jacket and blue ruffled shirt. His curly, sandy colored hair looked golden in the bright sunlight that was streaming through the stain-glass windows.

It was the first time I ever saw him in a pair of shiny black men's dress shoes. Even his socks matched. He was wearing black tuxedo pants with a dark stripe going down each side.

I guess this proves he really loves me, I thought. In the year I had come to know Gene I realized he never liked getting dressed up for anything. He preferred comfortable and informal clothes like jeans and turtle necks. As did I. I guess that was something else we had in common.

When Gene spotted us, he stopped pacing and instantly relaxed. I blew him a kiss. My two bridesmaids, Teddy and Sue, and my lovely maid of honor Ann were waiting in the lobby to greet me. They all looked beautiful in their colorful summer dresses. Ann was especially pretty in a blue silk gown that flowed gracefully around her tall slim figure.

Friends were beginning to make their way into the pews when Reverend Kellerman appeared, followed by two men, one wheeling in a baby grand piano, the other walking over to Gene and shaking his hand. He was very handsome and looked familiar but I couldn't place him at that moment.

"Don't be nervous, Sweetheart," my father whispered as piano music began to play *Come Saturday Morning*. It was our cue to begin. As we walked down the aisle I felt like I was dreaming as I listened to the lyrics of that song

Come Saturday Morning
I'm going away with my friend.
We'll Saturday spend
More than half of the day,
Just I and my friend,
We'll travel for miles in our Saturday smiles,
'And then we'll remember
Long after Saturday's gone.

When we reached the altar, my father let go of my hand and stepped aside. Gene sprang to my side and we both began to laugh.

"I have a surprise for you," he said.

Reverend Kellerman, looking quite pleased, announced that Gene had written a song for me and that his good friend, Edward Mellindick, a Broadway actor was now currently starring in the production, "A Man with a Load of Mischief" would sing it.

"It's called **"Patti's Wedding Song."**

Ed walked over to the piano and began to sing in a rich warm baritone:

As waves roll in from the sea
This June-kissed morning
To race up the beach
Then seaweed creep
In all her majesty,
The sea is warning,
The secret of love,
Lies in the deep.
The Sea rolls on endlessly
Not hinting that she
Knows love is the mystery,
The world dreams of
And so on our wedding day,
I sing to Patti,
The wonderment of our gift of love.

I was overwhelmed. So many sensations were hitting me I couldn't totally focus. I was just swept away, speechless and unsteady.

I could hear a few people in the pews behind me whispering, "That was so beautiful" and "what a beautiful song." I think some of them might have applauded if they weren't in church.

I squeezed Gene's hand and thanked him for such a lovely gift. He was beaming and kept rocking back and forth on his feet as he was wont to do every time he too was overwhelmed with happiness.

As Ed approached us, we shook hands and congratulated him for singing so well.

"My pleasure," he said. "It's a great song written by a great guy."

When it came time to exchange our rings, Kellerman asked if anyone present knew any reason why Gene and I should not be wed.

I held my breath, hoping my mother had not hopped the train and was about to come bounding down the aisle. When all was silent, I let out a sigh of relief and winked at Gene.

"Let us now proceed," Kellerman said.

He turned to me.

"Pat, do you take this man, Eugene C. Flinn to be your lawful husband?"

"Yes," I said, pausing to savor the sacredness of the moment.

When he asked Gene if he would accept me as his wife, Gene said for all the church and neighborhood to hear, "Yes, I do and I will forever."

"I now pronounce you man and wife," Kellerman smiled, hugging me and shaking Gene's hand.

We kissed and held each other, knowing we would treasure this moment for the rest of our lives.

I turned and looked into my father's eyes. He was smiling and gave me a big thumb's up.

"Two love birds," he said. "Too bad King Farouk missed this. I'm sure one day she will regret it."

Karen Carpenter's hit song, "We're Only Just Begun," was starting to play from the church's stereo system as we walked down the aisle, greeting friends, shaking hands, and throwing kisses.

Gene suggested we take a few photos in Central Park to capture the beauty of the day and our moment in the sun. Friends snapped away with their cameras and videos as we posed and kissed under trees and on park benches and along winding leafy paths meandering through the green meadows and cinder paths.

Eventually it was time to hop into the yellow submarine waiting for us in front of the church. Tim, Gene's son who was also his best man, didn't have a license yet, but he somehow managed to retrieve it from a nearby parking garage and was gallantly holding open the passenger-side door for me.

"Away we go," I laughed, waving good-bye to all our friends. "See you all down at the shore."

I kissed my father good-bye as he puffed away on a Lucky Strike cigarette.

"You told me you were quitting," I scolded.

"I take only a few drags and then throw it away."

"A few drags can still kill you," I warned.

"Not on your wedding day," he laughed. "Relax, Baby Doll, and drive safely."

My hair and white lacy veil were blowing in the wind as the yellow submarine made its way to Bricktown.

We didn't have a *Just Wed* sign on the rear bumper, but cars going by were beeping their horns and waving as they saw us speeding by in our open convertible.

Gene had ordered a wedding cake from a local bakery just outside Brick, so we stopped to pick it up.

"Where are we going to put it?" I asked glancing at the back seat which was so small it might not hold a tiny hatbox.

"You'll have to hold it on your lap. It's not that far."

When Gene returned carrying the cake, the box looked about three feet tall.

"Hold it tight," he warned. "We don't want it smashed since it has two nice statues of a bride and groom on top."

"If you stop short, the marriage is over," I joked. "I'll be the first bride in history to be buried alive by her own wedding cake."

Paul was in the kitchen basking two big turkeys when we arrived. He kissed me and shook Gene's hand.

There was a delicious aroma of roasting turkey and potatoes, frying onions and peppers, and warm baking bread.

Since neither Gene nor I had eaten anything that morning, we were starving. Paul made us turkey sandwiches on thick crusty bread with mayonnaise and pickles and as we sat down to eat, it hit me how blessed I was to savor these precious moments of my life.

Soon our guests would be here with us, but it was sheer joy to sit there with Gene and for the first time eat together as man and wife.

By the time we finished, several of our guests arrived and the party began.

Some folks wandered out to the patio to watch the river; others lingered in the living room, drinking wine and beer and listening to music while they chatted with one another. Tim sat with my three friends, shamelessly flirting with them. Around I p.m. I began to worry because my father still hadn't arrived, but just as I was about to call home, he came walking in with a woman.

At first I didn't know who this woman was or why he had bought her along, but as I approached them, I realized she was my former chemistry teacher at Sacred Heart Academy, Sister Mary Katherine.

"Congratulations on your marriage," she said. "You must be wondering why I am dressed in this skirt and blouse and not wearing my nun's garb."

"Yes, Sister, I didn't recognize you immediately."

"Well, big surprise! I'm no longer a nun. I left the convent, so please don't call me sister anymore. I prefer to be addressed by my name Katherine."

"Well, Katherine, I am very happy for you. Looks like we're both starting a whole new way of life."

"Yes, isn't it wonderful," she smiled. "We never know where life will take us. I'm working with a social service agency in Hoboken now finding shelter for homeless families."

"That's wonderful," I said. "But leaving the convent after so many years must be a big adjustment for you."

"Yes, it is. But I couldn't be happier. I discovered my real self and I'm free at last."

Years later I thought a lot about that brief encounter. It was simple and yet profound. If our lives can change so quickly who are we? How do we define ourselves? We are not our names, our past histories, or who other people think we are. *Know thyself*, Socrates warned. But who or what is this real self? It left me wondering. Maybe that is why the book Gene was carrying when I first saw him left such an impression on me—*I'm Not Stiller* about a man in search of his real self. He has shed his old identity and despite so much pressure by former friends and family he had refused to accept their definition of him.

Katherine and I talked for a long time until my father returned carrying two glasses of white wine. He handed one to Katherine and one to me.

"I figured since you're not a nun anymore, you might like a drink now," he said. "Enjoy!"

I asked Katherine how she ran into my father.

"I was waiting for the bus on Washington Street to take me into New York City when your dad stopped his car and said hello. He said he recognized me from the night he prevented his cop friends from arresting me."

She laughed.

"I was protesting the war and when a cop arrived he told me to leave because I was a disgrace to the church. I got so mad I swung my protest sign at him. I didn't hit him but he got so mad he grabbed me and began cuffing me for arrest. Fortunately, your father happened to be there, saw what was happening and managed to calm the cop down telling him he would go to hell if he arrested a nun."

"That cop wasn't the brightest bulb in the house," my father said with a shrug. "I'm sure he still believes in Santa Claus."

The party was in full swing at that point as people began to fill their plates with Paul's delicious turkey and trimmings.

I was surprised when there was a sudden commotion at the front door. I looked up and saw Gene's former friend, Bill Rosenberry stumble in with his buddy Charlie the Madman. I knew Gene had not invited them since he knew they could be a problem. They always showed up drunk at parties and refused to leave. Somehow Rosenberry had heard about the wedding and simply invited himself and the Madman.

They arrived with three dozen cans of Foster Ale and took little time finishing them off along with plenty of Paul's turkey sandwiches. Charlie, who weighed over 300 pounds, had lots of practice eating. His jaws were like a garbage compressor and along with the turkey he ate piles of potatoes, stuffing, and bread.

After a good hour or so of drinking, they were a mess. Gene did his best to get rid of them but they just ignored him and carried on like drunken teenage boys at a frat party.

My father, who had been watching them for some time, was determined to help Gene out.

He strolled over to Fat Charlie and flashed his fireman's badge. Rosenberry and Charlie were so drunk they thought it was a policeman's badge.

"You guys leave now or I'll call for backup and have you both arrested for disorderly conduct. Understand?"

As drunk as they were, Charlie wanted no business with cops since he had numerous outstanding tickets for drunken driving and disorderly conduct.

Grabbing hold of his beer, Charlie staggered to the door with Rosenberry reluctantly following close behind.

We thought our troubles were over once they were in the driveway, but before anyone could stop him Charlie the Madman wandered over to the statue of the Blessed Mother that was on the front lawn and with one fierce kick knocked it flying. If fell on the pavement shattering into little pieces. Gene and I were shocked but there was little we could do just then except call the cops to let them know two drunken men were driving in an old grey Oldsmobile through the streets of Bricktown.

"Don't worry about that statue." my father said, trying to perk us up." This is your wedding day. I'll find some glue tomorrow and piece it back together again. No one will know the difference."

"I promised Mrs. Trumley that nothing would be damaged. I have to tell her the truth. If we can't repair it, I will buy her another one."

"Well maybe it ain't that expensive. I think you would have to pay a lot more if it were a statue of Jesus."

Gene and I laughed so hard, we almost forgot the damage.

By the time we returned to the house, Mrs. Hillock, the mother of my friend, Teddy, was in the kitchen with Paul, wanting to know where her daughter had gone.

"I haven't seen her in some time now and I'm getting a bit worried. It's not like Teddy to just disappear."

Paul, who had a few beers by this time, was not very helpful.

"Zoom, Zoom," was all he could say in response.

I tried to reassure the woman Teddy was probably outside admiring the river.

Gene escorted her back to her seat and brought her a large slice of wedding cake, but she declined saying the cake was too unwieldy to eat nicely since it hadn't been professionally cut.

"I'll eat it then," Paul said, grabbing hold of the plate and stuffing the cake into his mouth.

I went looking for Teddy. As I approached the water, I saw Tim wearing only boxer shorts. He was bouncing up and down in the river, along with my three bridesmaids who had all shed their dresses and were swimming and cavorting merrily in their bras and panties. Teddy, her hair wringing wet, was laughing so hard people could hear her across the road.

I knew Mrs. Hillock would be shocked so I kept quiet about finding Teddy dancing in the river in her underwear.

Around 7 p.m. people began to leave.

"I told them it was getting late and time to go," my father said. "If I didn't they would have stayed all night."

"Thanks, Mick. We appreciate that."

"No problem. This is your time now."

"Thanks for everything, Dad. You really help us out in so many ways."

"I'm always in your corner, Patsy Doll."

Just then Katherine wandered over. She seemed a bit tipsy after drinking two glasses of wine.

"Your delightful father has offered to drive me home now," she said, patting me on the shoulder. "He's an angel, as you must know."

"Yes," I replied, hugging her. "He sure is."

"Nice meeting you," she said, shaking Gene's hand. "Enjoy your honeymoon."

She flashed the peace sign as she headed out the door with my father and Paul.

We watched the last car pull away. It contained my three bridesmaids and Tim, all of whom were still pretty damp but elated from their river frolic. Teddy's mother was driving and she didn't seem too happy to see Tim sitting so close to her daughter in the back seat.

Gene and I embraced once everyone was gone.

"It was a beautiful day," Gene whispered into my ear. "In fact, it was the best day of my life. I will never forget it."

"Neither will I," I replied. "I love you, Gene."

Outside the bedroom windows, early evening was sketching the last rays of the sun across the orange and red sky. Birds were singing their good-night melodies as the faithful old Matedeconk River flowed merrily along to the tune of passing time.

CHAPTER FIFTEEN

Quantum Leaps

*That it will never come again is what
makes life sweet. Emily Dickinson*

THE NEXT MORNING when I opened my eyes, I saw Gene smiling down at me.

"Now I don't have to take you home to Hoboken anymore. Now we can play together all day."

"And now Sister Madeline can't get me," I laughed. "I'm officially married and I can't be sent to the booby hatch without my husband's consent, and I'm pretty sure you won't agree to that, Gene."

A little later we showered together, but it was more hilarious than erotic. Gene kept dropping the soap, and I kept slipping on the shampoo and banging my elbow against the soap rack.

That was when Gene first began to notice what he called my *toilet tongue*. Whenever I injured myself in some way or dropped and broke something, I would curse like a seasoned sailor.

"It's hard to imagine my sweet little Tricia has such words in her vocabulary. And to think you went to Catholic schools run by nuns. I bet they would be horrified and shocked if they heard you now."

That first shower together became a wonderful memory along with so many others.

Later that morning we sat on the deck overlooking the river and ate our breakfast of scrambled eggs and toast. It was another beautiful early June day filled with warm sunlight and soft sea-scented breezes.

I remember Gene talking about all the lovely towns and villages that he had visited on his several trips to Europe as a chaperone for undergraduates who signed up for a two-week summer vacation abroad sponsored by the college. I had never been to Europe and it was exciting to hear him describe in such vivid detail the sights and sounds of these places.

"I remember seeing this gorgeous old houseboat festooned with flowers and sweet-smelling herbs on one of those old canals that winds its way through Amsterdam. There was a fat little man reclining on a blue and gold deck lounge reading Baudelaire's poems, *The Flowers of Evil.* He was smoking a pipe and he looked so involved with his book, I wanted to read it too. That's why I later assigned it in my lit classes."

'I'm glad you did. I had never heard of Baudelaire before, and I found some of his poems confusing and ambiguous, but they forced me to think about that grey area that falls between the *so-called* good and evil labels man places upon things."

"*There is nothing good or bad, but thinking makes it so.*" That's from Hamlet, right, Gene?"

He smiled at me.

"If only you were as smart in geography as you are in literature. By the way, what is the capital of Norway?"

"Copenhagen."

"Congratulations. A+"

"You forget I haven't had many opportunities to travel beyond Hoboken."

"Well, I promise we will do a lot of traveling in the years to come. We'll go to Paris, travel across England, Ireland and Wales, and buy a Europass so we can visit Germany, Austria, Norway and Sweden."

"Wonderful, but in the meantime, tell me this. Where shall we go today?'

A light breeze caressed us as we sat and watched the morning light dapple the grass and trees.

"Well, I know you love horses, so how about going to the race track. Monmouth Raceway is nearby."

"Great idea."

"How about we call your father and Paul and see if they want to join us? I know they both love to gamble."

"Another great idea. I'll give my father a call now.

While we waited for them to arrive, Gene and I prepared lunch.

We found a portable cooler in the garage and filled it with ice. We had lots of turkey left over so I made sandwiches while Gene made ice tea. His ice tea was so delicious it became my favorite beverage summer or winter.

By the time we cleaned up the kitchen, Mick and Paul were arriving. The old Rambler backfired as it turned into the driveway so I knew they were here.

"Hello, Lovebirds," Paul said. "I hope your happiness brings us luck at the track."

"I dreamed three numbers last night," I announced. "9-1-3. Maybe you should bet on those. Dreams should not be taken lightly."

"If we hurry and are in time for the first race, I'll buy a 9-1-3 trifecta and hope for the best," my father said, giving me a quick hug.

All the way to the race-track Mick talked about the weather. He was trying to figure out which horses performed the best under sunny skies and mild temperatures.

"George Boy likes muddy tracks. I've been following him in the scratch sheets and when it rains, he comes in first or second. On a sunny day like today he'll probably be third or fourth. I think I'll have to go for Strong Man who loves hotter temps."

We turned right at the blinking white arrow pointing to the entrance of Monmouth Raceway and drove along with fifty other cars into the immense overcrowded parking area. A young man wearing a bright orange jacket was waving his arms directing traffic right and left.

We were ushered into a spot almost a quarter of a mile from the front gate.

"Jesus," my father, exclaimed to the young parking attendant. "Can't we get a spot a little closer? We got some heavy stuff to carry. And besides this is my daughter and son-in-law's honeymoon, and it would be nice if you could give them a break."

"I wish I could, Sir, but as you can see it's a lovely day for walking. This is as close as you can get in this jammed parking area."

Mick pulled a five dollar bill from his pants' pocket and pressed it into the young man's hands.

"Go buy yourself a soda, kid."

"No thank you, Sir. I can't accept money. I could get fired."

"Nobody's looking, kid."

"I can't accept this, Sir.

He thrust the bill back into Mick's hand.

"O.K. I guess we will just have to hike it then."

Gene and Mick took hold of the ice cooler and began trudging along. Paul and I followed close behind.

Fortunately there was still time to place Mick's Trifecta when we arrived at the front ticket booth.

"This is so much fun," Gene said, putting his arm around me. "I couldn't be any happier. Here I am with my lovely wife, looking at beautiful horses under beautiful blue skies on a beautiful summer day."

"You're on your honeymoon," Mick smiled. "Maybe you guys will bring me luck."

Soon the horses were led into the starting gate, their jockeys looking quite spiffy in bright yellow, orange, green, and blue silk uniforms. I thought of Carson McCullers story, *The Jockey*. There is something very magical and mysterious about the bond between a human being and a powerful animal like a horse. They communicate without words and merge as one as they fly through time and space together.

I mentioned these thoughts to Gene, as we talked about Carson McCullers. Suddenly we heard the shout," *And they're off*" booming through a nearby loud speaker.

Mick and Paul were on their feet mesmerized by the speeding horses as they raced neck and neck. I couldn't see the number on each horse, but when I heard the announcer say that number 9, a horse named *Believe It In* was leading, I began to pay more attention.

Believe It In was charging like a demon around the sharp turns, doing his best to keep the lead as several other horses were closing in.

When the home stretch was in sight, *Believe It In* and his jockey surged ahead in an incredible burst of energy, crossing the finish line in a hurricane of sweat, mud, and tears.

Gene and I were ecstatic, carrying on like two kids who had been on the winning team in a Little League game.

My father was more casual. It was obvious he was happy that his horse had won but he also seemed embarrassed by our excitement.

"Calm down, you guys," he whispered, glancing right and left, "We don't want to look like a bunch of amateurs here. And we don't want to attract attention and get robbed of our winnings in the parking lot later."

We promised we would behave ourselves, but when the next race began and it looked like a horse named Spartan was beginning to surge from behind and race head to head with Best Bet, we got excited again. Spartan's number was *one* and if he won, it would mean, I had correctly dreamed two of the numbers in the Trifecta.

Win he did, ten to one in a hair's finish. Mick seemed slightly more excited than before. Paul raised his beer in salute to the horse and then took a long swig.

We found it hard to believe when the third race began and our horse Razor's Edge, number three, another long shot, held onto the lead going down the final ten yards and crossing the finish line in a flash of color, vibration, and thundering sound.

Mick was big winner. Over a thousand bucks. Gene wanted to celebrate by picnicking under a tree next to the stables so we could see all the horses return to their stables.

Mick wanted to keep betting since he believed he was now on a winner's streak. I was afraid he would lose all his winnings, but I didn't want to tell him what to do. He had allowed me to make my own decisions about marriage, and so I wanted to give him the same respect and freedom to be himself regardless of the outcome.

We were all exhausted driving home after such an exciting day. Gene and I wanted Mick and Paul to stay the night and not drive back to Hoboken. Fortunately, they agreed. We sat up late in the cool of the backyard watching the moonlight do a little dance across the black waters of the river while we talked late into the evening.

My father was clearly enjoying himself. I could tell he was at peace and ruminating.

"That river and those trees were here when George Washington was alive," he said. "And they will be here long after we are all gone. Makes you think. But I'm a realist. One generation goes and then another takes its place. Nothing we can do to stop the march of time. It reminds me of a big wheel. We all go around for a while and then we all start falling off and disappearing, one by one."

"Do you think it makes any sense?" Gene asked, draping his arm around my shoulder. We were sitting so close, it was hard to tell our bodies apart.

"Our human brains can't comprehend it all. It's just too deep. Too far beyond our ideas. But right now we are sitting here, all happy and healthy and that's the only thing that matters."

Paul began to hum something that sounded like **The Battle Hymn of the Republic.** Then he fell asleep mumbling "Zoom, Zoom, Zoom."

The next morning we were all bleary-eyed until we had our coffee and breakfast. Paul took charge of the kitchen, whipping up a big bowl of scrambled eggs. The coffee smelled like heaven and slowly I began to wake up.

After breakfast we washed the dishes and cleaned up the kitchen. I could tell it was going to be a warmer day than yesterday and I was contemplating a nice swim in the river or a refreshing stroll along the beach. My father ventured outside to look under the hood of his old Rambler to check the oil. Gene and I were reading the paper when suddenly my father came running in.

"Gene. There's a couple out there who wants to know what happened to the statue."

"What statue?" Gene asked.

"The statue of Mary. That jerk Charlie what's his name smashed it, remember?"

Gene and I knew at once trouble was about to drop like a truckload of bricks on our heads. We dashed to the door.

A man and woman in their late sixties or early seventies were standing in front of the shattered statue, staring down at it. They looked as if they were about to cry.

"Hello," Gene said. "May I help you?"

"Yes," the man replied, pointing to the broken pieces, "What happened here?"

"Are you friends of Mrs. Trumley?"

"I'm her sister Elizabeth. And this is my husband, Thomas."

"I'm Gene and this is my wife, Tricia."

We all shook hands.

"As you may know we are renting this house for a week and unfortunately a very immature person arrived uninvited to our gathering and broke it when we asked him to leave. I realize we are responsible for this damage and I will pay Mrs. Trumley to have it repaired or replaced," Gene said.

"We don't want it replaced," Thomas snapped. "This statue was made by an artist for our daughter who was very ill at the time. Mrs. Trumley gave it to us so we could pray for our daughter's recovery. We had to leave it here when we moved from our house into an apartment. But we come every weekend to say a prayer in thanks."

"Is your daughter well now?"

"Yes," Elizabeth replied. "Our lady answered our prayers. Sue Ann is thirty-five and has three children."

"Well, we will do everything we can to have it fully restored."

My father reappeared holding a large tub of Elmer's glue in his hands.

"Don't worry, folks. I'll work on this right away. I'm pretty good at fixing broken dishes since my wife is always throwing them at me."

Gene and I started to laugh but thought better when we saw Thomas looking aghast.

"Thanks, Mick, but we'll have it professionally restored for these nice people," Gene announced.

"Unfortunately, the artist who made this statue has passed away," Elizabeth said. "You will have to find someone else to do the job."

After they finally left Gene and I hurried into the house and spent the morning searching the telephone book for local art restorers. We finally found a man in Seaside Heights who agreed to take a look and see what could be done.

He arrived in the late afternoon in a fire-engine red Volkswagen camper with a large For Sale sign in the side window. He looked like a hippy who had wandered in from the 60s'.

"Peace," he said, extending his hand. Large hand-painted rings sat on four of his five fingers. "Jake's the name. What can I do for you?"

We pointed to the broken statue. "We need it restored."

Jake was silent while he examined a few pieces.

"This little lady sure has taken a beating," he mused. "What happened? Someone had a bad trip or something."

We laughed and began to relax with Jake's off-beat sense of humor.

"Yes, a former friend, high on drugs, attacked it in a rage when we asked him to leave this house."

"Well, you're lucky he attacked a statue and not you."

"Yes, you're right," Gene replied. "But this statue doesn't belong to us. We're renting this house for a week and promised the owner we would repair any damage to the property."

"Why not just buy a new statue? All these Blessed Mothers look alike to me."

"The owner has a sentimental attachment to this one. It's a long story, believe me."

"No doubt about that. As John Lennon once said, *whatever helps you through the night.*"

"So, do you think you can repair this?" I asked.

"Honestly, this job is going to be major brain surgery for me, but I'm up to it, if you are."

"If you do a good job, maybe we will buy your camper as a thank you. I see it's for sale."

"Terrific," Jake said, shaking Gene's hand. "I'll do my best."

After he gathered up the pieces, Jake climbed into his VW and took off, *Dust in the Wind* blasting from his stereo.

That night sitting on the patio and watching the stars glowing over our little spot of earth, we wondered what would have happened if Jake were stopped by a cop on his way home. How would he ever explain a beheaded Blessed Mother in his back seat?

Two days later we were enjoying lunch in the kitchen when we heard the camper pull into the driveway. We watched as Jake, smoking a weed carried a fully restored statue in his arms.

There before our eyes was a lovely work of art. Not only were all the sundry pieces in place without a trace of glue or a disfiguring scar, but the colors on Mary's gown and slippers radiated a brilliance and living energy hard to describe. She truly looked resurrected. Her eyes, deep blue, purple and penetrating seemed ethereal.

"Jake, you did a remarkable job," Gene exclaimed. "How did you manage to do this?"

"With a little help from my friends," he shrugged, holding up his reefer and pulling a small bottle of pink pills from his pocket. "Grass, LSD and a little imagination work wonders. Everything is energy, man. Energy, frequency, and vibration make this world we inhabit go round and round. And different frequencies have different colors. By mixing dark ones with lighter ones you get balance, harmonic balance or a kind of living light."

Neither of us understood what he was saying but it was interesting just the same.

"Besides, I was listening to the Beatles while I was tripping and *Let It Be*, my favorite song, started to play. I took that as a sign. *When I find myself in times of trouble, Mother Mary comforts me, speaking words of wisdom. Let it Be, Let it Be.*"

Years later Gene and I often wondered what happened to Jake, the Stoned Philosopher. Did he go the way of most hippies in the 60s and 70s or did he stay true to his spirit and live always in the moment?

We had a brief encounter that summer but one that was exhilarating and unforgettable. We decided to buy Jake's camper for $500 and we paid him $300 for repairing the statue. The last time we heard from him he told us he used the money to travel to India where he was studying with the Maharishi.

The camper became our first toy as a married couple.

"Let's plan on a trip to Vermont, "Gene said. "It'll be fun camping under the stars."

That afternoon we headed for the local Motor Vehicle office, registered the camper, attached the new license plates, and then drove to a nearby florist shop where we bought a big yellow sunflower which we attached to the antenna. Then, happy as teenagers going for their first joy ride in their father's car, we took turns driving our camper which we christened The Magical Mystery Bus through town.

Mick and Paul came to visit again a few days later along with some friends from the city. We sat on the patio and savored the fresh night air while we listened to the subtle music of the Metedeconk playing nearby. Above us the sky shone with ancient stars caressed by a sea of ever expanding space. For a little while as we all sat chatting and laughing, we forgot about the turmoil and pain that was raging in so many places on earth racked by violence, ignorance and poverty.

From an open window in the kitchen we could hear the radio playing *A Summer Place,* a song which even today takes me back to that wonderful first week as a married couple we spent in Brick Town New Jersey in 1971.

CHAPTER SIXTEEN

Frequency, Vibration, and Wave Fluctuation

Life is nothing without a little chaos to make it interesting. Amelia Atwater Rhodes

WHEN THE FOLLOWING Sunday morning arrived we said farewell to Mrs. Trumley lovely house and headed for Bentley Avenue in Jersey City where we would live in Gene's apartment. It was on the fifth floor in a well-kept Tutor-style building nearly a century old. It towered above the large, private homes with wrap-around porches, spacious interiors, and elegant old-world charm that dotted the tree-lined street.

From our bedroom window we could see into the backyards of these homes where there was plenty of space for overflowing flower and vegetable gardens and sun-kissed patios.

Our apartment seemed enormous to me. There were eight rooms: a spacious kitchen, living room, and four bedrooms. Large windows filled every room with light and airiness, even the two bathrooms. My favorite, the bathroom suite, had a big claw-foot tub, a four-jet tiled shower, and an Italian marble sink.

I loved the shower since it was large enough to accommodate six people. The only problem was that occasionally the water would shut off in the building and if one were soaped up in the shower and waiting to rinse in nice warm water, one would not be happy.

When Tim was showering and the water shut off, he would pound on the walls and scream bloody hell.

Naturally this was quite upsetting to the two elderly unmarried sisters who were living in the apartment directly below us.

In response to Tim's shouts, they would bang a broom against their ceiling to let us know they were not pleased with the noise.

I suspected they also did not approve of Gene with his wild hair and beard, and when they first saw me moving into the apartment with my suitcases, they probably thought the worst.

I smiled whenever we met in the elevator, and a few times I waved my wedding finger under their long noses but they simply stared straight ahead and showed no awareness of my presence.

The real scandal came, however, when we purchased a stationary exercise bike and set it up in the bedroom. Whenever I began to peddle hard, they would knock furiously against their ceiling with the heavy broom. No doubt they were shocked, picturing unimaginable erotic scenes in their uptight, puritan brains.

We both did our best to respect them since they had been living there for many years and had a right to remain content in their home. But there were times when circumstances occurred we could not control and they blamed us anyway.

One day when we were washing dishes the water suddenly shut off due to pressure problems.

We didn't turn off the faucet since we assumed the water would soon be flowing again and we could finish washing the dishes we had piled in the sink. The water remained off for much longer than we expected, however, and unfortunately we forgot about it.

After reading the Sunday papers and doing a few chores, we decided to go for a jog in Lincoln Park.

When we returned to the apartment about an hour later, we were surprised to see so many of our neighbors gathering in the hallway with the landlord, Mr. Darby who shouted an expletive when he saw us.

"Where were you? I've been trying to reach you. There's a flood inside your apartment. Water is pouring down into the apartments below you."

We rushed to open the front door. Water was pouring from the kitchen faucet and overflowing the sink onto the kitchen and living room floors.

Gene quickly turned off the faucet and thankfully the water stopped.

"You're responsible for this damage," Mr. Darby shouted. "Your negligence resulted in this horrible mess."

"Well, Mr. Darby, you're also responsible," I argued. "If you had corrected that water pressure problem we have been dealing with for some time now, this would not have happened."

"That is the fault of the city," he replied, glaring at me.

"As our landlord, you could have taken more aggressive actions or hired a plumber."

Mr. Darby threw up his hands in frustration.

"I am not made of money. You all think I am. But I am not. You neglected your faucet and now you must pay for these damages."

He ran down the stairs, anxious to make a quick getaway before we could reply.

For the rest of the day we mopped up water and threw out everything that was water-logged and damaged beyond repair.

The task we found most difficult, however, was facing the elderly sisters downstairs.

Late that afternoon we knocked on their door and apologized for what had happened.

"Naturally we will pay for any damages you may have incurred," Gene assured them, also offering to take them out to dinner that evening if they were unable to cook in their kitchen."

"No thank you" they said in unison. "We don't like eating out. Fortunately, we can manage here since our stove was not damaged by your negligence."

With that they slammed the door shut.

One of their neighbors, a young man named Tom, who had been wounded fighting in Viet Nam, saw what was happening.

"Not the friendliest gals in the building, are they?" he laughed.

After chatting a bit he invited us into his apartment to meet his wife Pam and to have a beer.

Pam was an attractive friendly woman just a few years older than I. Nevertheless, we had quite a few things in common. She and Tom recently married and were now attending college together. The three of us were English majors and enjoyed writing. Tom and Pam hoped to become journalists one day and travel the world as foreign correspondents.

We spent over an hour with them that afternoon and made plans to have dinner together at the Clam Broth House in Hoboken, a famous fish restaurant known world-wide.

What started out as a bad day became a good one since we found two new friends who were smart, witty, and lived only steps away.

I learned so many new things that first summer of our marriage. One of them was cooking. My mother had always done the cooking when I was a child and she never asked me to help her, so I never learned to do anything except occasionally boil an egg. When Paul was not around, Gene had to cook for himself so he learned how to make a few dishes. When I told him I too wanted to learn, he began showing me how to make mash potatoes, roasted chicken, beef stews, mushroom omelets, and some soups. His real specialty, however, was salad.

He would mix a big bowl of lettuce with just about anything he could find in the refrigerator. We used to have contests to see who could come closest to guessing the number of ingredients in a night's salad. It was usually pretty high since Gene's salads consisted of lettuce, apples, tomatoes, celery, avocados, mushrooms, croutons, basil, parsley, peppers, bits of bacon, chicken, tuna fish, peanuts, strawberries, peaches, and always blue cheese sprinkled generously throughout.

I loved Gene's crunchy refreshing salads especially on hot summer days, and I quickly learned to make them myself.

It was fun sitting in that cozy kitchen with the windows open on summer nights listening to the neighborhood kids playing baseball in the streets below as we prepared dinner.

The radio would be playing softly in the background, maybe a Carpenter tune, or something from **Sonny and Our Gang,** and we would sing along as we cut up the celery or peeled an apple. Gene loved their song, **Sunday Morning,** and he would belt it out for the whole neighborhood to hear.

Fortunately the two sisters downstairs never whacked the broom against the ceiling when he was singing. Maybe they secretly liked his strong male voice. I liked to imagine they were both secretly in love with him.

Although we were both enjoying life in that apartment, Gene loved to travel, so around the first week in August we decided to drive to New England and spend some time exploring a few scenic towns in Connecticut, New Hampshire, Vermont, and Maine.

I had never been to a bed and breakfast inn, but Gene loved them and wanted me to experience them too.

Our first stop was the Grafton Inn in Vermont. We chose that one because we heard it was the oldest operating inn in America, established in 1801. It was located right in Grafton Village's historic district, and we were not only excited to explore the town, but I was anxious to brush up on my history and get a taste for what life was like when stagecoaches delivered travelers across dusty roads to these comfortable inns after their long, tiresome journeys.

We were not disappointed. The inn itself was beautiful with a large porch where guests could sit and enjoy the morning sunlight and the soft evening twilights. The main room was spacious, and comfortably furnished with early American and English antiques, original oil paintings and family portraits.

An enormous fieldstone fireplace lent an old-world ambience to the room. People in the past not only warmed the house by these massive fireplaces, they also cooked and baked in them. I imagined the delightful smells of baking bread and home-made soup filling the old inn during frigid, snowy winters as weary travelers came in from the cold.

Upstairs each room was light, airy and cozy with fireplaces, wide-board pumpkin pine floors and oak ceiling beams. I had never been in a bedroom or home like this before and when I declared to Gene that I must have died and gone to heaven, he laughed.

We were enjoying a second honeymoon as we strolled hand in hand along the cobblestone streets of the historic village, visiting art galleries, wandering into tiny shops, having snacks in the Old Tavern, and sampling a variety of cheese in the famous Grafton Cheese shop.

In the middle of the afternoon the innkeeper served home-made cookies and English tea for the guests. Gene always liked relaxing with the **New York Times** or reading a book from the well-stocked library in the room next door.

It was fun talking to the other guests at breakfast. An elderly couple from Manhattan told us about the Weston Playhouse which was only a short drive away. They said they had seen **Next,** one-act comedy by Terence McNally playing there and it was very entertaining.

Since Gene and I both loved the theater, we bought tickets for that night's performance. We weren't disappointed. The actors were talented professionals, the direction was fast-paced, the set imaginative, and the costumes creative and colorful.

As we sat watching the production, we began to imagine owning a playhouse like Weston. Its building was a former courthouse with old-world elegance and charm. When the town of Weston converted it into the playhouse it managed to maintain that spirit.

Gene often talked about a book he loved called **Broadway in a Barn.** He was intrigued by the idea of a summer theater where traveling actors perform in a variety of plays as they do in English regional theaters.

Several years later when we were shopping for a house in the country we were fortunate to find just the home we wanted next to a community theater. That was when I seriously began thinking that dreams and imagination result in real material creation. In other words, our thoughts become our reality. Did that mean that I imagined Gene and he imagined me?

These questions we both enjoyed mulling over whenever we got the chance to sit quietly and ruminate together. The more time we spent together, we discovered the more things we had in common.

While in Vermont that first summer we learned we both loved visiting historic General Stores. We loved seeing how people lived and shopped when there were no supermarkets or malls and certainly no large crowds pushing and shoving their way through narrow, cramped aisles.

Low crooked ceilings, old weathered beams, and creaky wooden floors were part and parcel of every store, and we loved them. We also loved the big brass antique cash registers with their push down numbered keys at the front check-out counter, and the way store clerks would wrap up purchases in sheets of heavy brown paper tied with string dangling from a ceiling hook.

Many of the General Stores we visited that summer displayed old treasures like antique women's leather boots, heavy cauldrons, and dried herbs that lent a sweet strong aroma to the room. It was a step back in time with no ATM machines, plastic credit cards, or self-check out counters. Instead the store clerk would add up your purchases by removing a pencil behind his ear and writing figures on little sheets of paper that could also serve as I.O.U's in case you were short of cash and needed credit.

The Vermont General Store we visited that summer was no exception. We strolled around eying all the goodies: fresh made jams bottled and ready for sale on shelves; maple syrup; blueberry pancake mix; glass jars filled with sweet peaches swimming in thick syrup just waiting to be sampled.

The delicious mouth watering aroma of strawberry muffins and chocolate chip scones baking in the oven was enticing, so we bought a dozen which we ate over the course of two days as we said good-bye to Vermont at the end of our short vacation and headed back home.

That summer I got to better know Gene's children. I was twenty and not experienced at all in mothering, but eventually we all became family and I liked to think of myself as their big sister and friend.

They were part of Gene and since I loved Gene, how could I not love them too?

On weekends when they visited we would go bike riding in Central Park or ice skating at Rockafellar Center. It was especially exciting to visit the city during Christmas holidays when snow was in the air and bright cheery lights illuminated store fronts and streets.

One day in late autumn when the kids were visiting, I decided to invite my mother and father to meet them. Although it was a bit awkward at first for my mother, her motherly instincts slowly kicked in and I was astonished when she later confessed she liked them all very much and thought them beautiful, lovely children.

As Neville Goddard, teacher, mystic, and author once wrote, *"Miracles never cease to happen."* If my mother could change her mind, anything was possible.

CHAPTER SEVENTEEN

Electromagnetic High-Energy Exchanges

The only thing more dangerous than ignorance is arrogance. Einstein

TOWARD THE END of July Gene decided to take the kids to a college town for a week's vacation so they could get a taste of what campus life was like. After doing some research, he chose to rent a small apartment in a house belonging to Dartmouth College in Hanover, New Hampshire.

It was actually a fraternity house during the school year, but in the summer it became a guest house for visitors who wanted to explore the campus and the small village of Hanover.

When we arrived with four of Gene's youngest children, -- the other kids were either working summer jobs or vacationing with the families of their friends--, we were greeted by a young guy who we later learned was the running back for Dartmouth's football team.

He certainly looked like a football player. He was six foot six and weighted about two hundred and twenty pounds, all of which was solid muscle. He was good-looking in an all American boy way with sandy hair, blue eyes, and a big bright smile.

He told us that he lived on the top floor and was hired by the college to make sure that all guests were comfortable and safe during their stay. It was hard to believe that anyone would feel unsafe in quiet little Hanover, but it was nice to know that he would be available if we ran into problems or had any questions about something in the house.

His name was Bill Tanner, and he and Gene hit it off very well, talking about football, and political science which he was majoring in. The only thing that Gene didn't know at the time was how competitive Bill was when it came to playing chess, a game he obviously loved and was exceptionally good at.

Almost every night after dinner and a leisurely stroll through Hanover Square, eating ice cream cones, we would return home to find Bill waiting at the kitchen table with the chess board all set up and ready to go.

Most nights Gene felt like playing, even though he had lost the first two games. But there were some nights when he just wanted to relax, talk, or read a book. But he always agreed to play to keep Bill happy. On the third and fourth night Gene won, capturing Bill's King and Queen and announcing "Checkmate."

The kids, who had been watching intensely, began dancing up and down, cheering loudly. Bill was pretty surprised and also a little upset, but he tried to put a good face on things.

From that night on, however, Bill was determined to win, not only in chess but in debates over politics, history, religion, science and any subject that happened to come up at the breakfast table, or at night after the chess game.

I had never seen such a competitive guy, and he soon began to annoy me. I thought he was conceited, and I wondered if many athletes and privileged ivy leaguers were as self-absorbed.

Gene, being a lot kinder than I, was only amused by Bill's behavior.

Every night for the remainder of our week's vacation, Bill pestered Gene to play. Sometimes Gene won, but if he lost, he laughed and never seemed to get rattled.

When Bill lost, it was a different story. He would sit pouting and shaking his head like someone whose pockets had just been picked. It didn't help when the kids teased him calling him a sore loser and a big baby.

Personally, I wanted to say the same thing as the kids, but Gene told me to *"rise above it,"* like the Christian Scientists.

It was another wonderful revelation about Gene's character and personality.

There was not a mean streak in his body.

When Bill left us alone during the day, we had plenty of time to go hiking, biking, canoeing, and swimming in the Olympic size pool at the Fitness Gym on campus.

No matter how many double-dip ice cream cones we all ate during that vacation, none of us gained weight since we were so active during the day. We jogged, swam, and walked for miles every day.

Most mornings we had the pool entirely to ourselves since there were so few students on campus. The kids especially loved the water and would race around each other, splashing and jumping and carrying on like a school of playful dolphins having fun in the sun.

One day, however, after some rough play, little Celine wound up with a broken wrist after she fell on the slippery deck trying to escape her big sister who was chasing her with a water balloon.

We spent the afternoon in a nearby hospital where doctors set her wrist and then put her arm in a cast. She was a brave little girl and didn't even cry, although the pain must have been intense.

Unfortunately that accident ended all our visits to the swimming pool, but Celine didn't seem to mind too much because after leaving the hospital we all went for pizza and ice cream and pretty soon things were back to normal.

One day we visited Dartmouth's well-stocked library where it was a joy just to wander among the impressive stacks and tall rows of book.

While the kids explored the children's section, Gene and I sat in comfortable armchairs reading the local papers and catching up on the national news from the *Times*.

On other afternoons if it rained, and we didn't feel like driving around the countryside, we would visit several bookstores in the village square. Some of them were second hand shops and since the books were so inexpensive, we usually left with a dozen or so.

Gene was always encouraging his kids to read, and he would play games with them to name an author or a character from one of their favorite books or classics. He would also try to teach them French and Spanish by playing games and making up sentences with each word.

The kids enjoyed these games, and besides making them a little smarter, they made us all more relaxed and at ease with one another.

Like everything in life, our week's vacation in Hanover came to an end and before we knew it, we were packing our bags and heading for home again.

Bill was there to say good-bye. He shook hands with everyone and said that he wished we would return again some day. I don't know if he really liked us, or whether he just wanted another week of chess with a partner who challenged him, but it was a nice send off, and we were happy, but also a little sad at having such a interesting vacation come to an end.

Years later, I would look back on those days and think how lucky I was to have experienced such moments. It was truly a dream come alive that unfolded in ways I never could have imagined when I was a child growing up. These memories live in my soul now, part of my eternal consciousness that will never die.

CHAPTER EIGHTEEN

The First Law of Thermodynamics

A ship is always safe at the shore, but that's
not what it's built for. Einstein

ONCE WE WERE home we had to adjust to the heat and humidity of city life again. The cool pleasant evenings in Hanover were replaced by hot stuffy days and nights in the busy city.

Although we had a reliable and efficient air conditioner in the apartment, stepping outside the building was like stepping into a steam room.

It was exceptionally humid all through July, and most of August, so we tried to run early in the morning under the shade of trees in Lincoln Park.

Running together had become our ritual. It gave us a chance to enjoy nature and conversation as we made our way around the cinder paths that circled the park's lake and grassy fields. It was so much nicer listening to the songs of birds than the noisy backfires of boulevard buses and speeding trucks.

After lunch Gene and I wrote together. We were working on three one act plays that were going to be staged and performed by his drama students at Rutgers University in September. Although he was teaching only part time as an adjunct professor there, the drama department agreed to allow him space in one of the university's off campus sites in Jersey City on Sip Avenue.

It was a fairly large space with enough room to hold about 100 people safely. Although technically it was not equipped as a theater, Gene was ready to set up a lighting booth, a performing space, and an adequate sound system. His intention was to enlist students as backstage carpenters, technicians, and prop people to assist in the production for college credit and experience.

My play was entitled *"Please Pass the Wheat Germ,"* a comedy about the encounter between a health fanatic and a chain smoking overweight slob who runs a broken down diner known for the highest number of cardio attacks occurring in a restaurant.

Gene's play, *"Big Day At Shea,"* was based on Steve Allen's short story, *The Public Hating.* It was about the powers of mind to both create and destroy, and the ways in which people can be influenced by political propaganda and mass hysteria. It was a brilliant play that had an immense impact on my thinking about the link between mind and matter. This led to my interest in Quantum Mechanics, and what physicists were discovering about reality and our role in shaping it.

Steve Allen agreed to read Gene's play when it was completed, and if he approved it, he would give us permission to perform it. We were both excited by this and spent a lot of time working on dialogue and scene development.

At night we would read aloud what we had written and make changes if one of us suggested something.

Time, as Einstein discovered, is relative. He tried explaining this theory by pointing out that an hour seems like an eternity when one is in a hospital waiting for an operation; whereas an hour seems like a second when one is talking to a beautiful woman.

Time for us that summer was like superman: faster than a speeding bullet.

Yes, we were technically still on our honeymoon and enjoying all the newness and bliss of married love, but we also had plenty of mundane things to do. By the time we ran, wrote, read, cooked, cleaned, shopped, played with the kids, and visited friends, it was time for bed.

Some days were hard to keep track of, especially when the kids came to visit and our regular routine was thrown off base. Mick and Paul would often drop by for a few hours and sometimes my mother would accompany them.

She seemed to like Paul because he kidded with her and made her feel relaxed. She didn't say it, but I think she was also impressed by the size of the apartment and the fact that it had an elevator. I could tell that she was also beginning to feel more comfortable and at ease with Gene.

It helped that he really liked my mother and understood her fears and concerns for my well-being. Gene had a great sense of humor and knew how to kid without hurting someone's feelings.

By mid August we were all beginning to feel like family, and so Gene decided that it might be a good idea before school began to have a vacation with Paul, the kids, and my parents. It would mean finding and renting another house large enough to accommodate everyone comfortably.

"Where would you like to go?" Gene asked, as one night. He had been studying a few guide books on New England.

"I'd love to visit Maine," I said. "It has so many things to offer. A great sea coast, rugged hills, spectacular views, cool summer weather, nice little towns, and delicious seafood."

"Maine, it is then," Gene agreed. "We'll leave one day this week to check out places."

We left that Thursday, August 11, 1971, a little after 9 A.M. in our yellow submarine, traveling north on I-95, pass New Haven, Worcester, Massachusetts, and Portsmouth, New Hampshire.

We stopped in Portsmouth for lunch and were so charmed by Market Square, we spent the rest of the day and night there.

After discovering a little French Bistro on Market Street, we couldn't resist the urge to sample their French onion soup and fresh fillets poached *Vin Blanc.*

A waiter dressed in the traditional white shirt, black pants, and black apron escorted us to a table by a window, took our order, and wished us a pleasant *bon appétit!*

I was improving not only my French, but also my taste in fine cuisine.

After such a delicious feast, we needed to work off some calories by strolling along the Portsmouth Harbor Trail, a scenic route with views of the harbor, the beach, the old drawbridge, the historic mansions, parks, and lovely old neighborhoods filled with 17th century buildings and homes.

There were also plenty of opportunities to stop and browse in antique shops, bookstores, and cafes that we discovered along the way.

We were walking for almost an hour when we came upon a lovely colonial inn directly across from the entrance to Prescott Park. A large white sign in front of the inn indicated that rooms were available on a nightly and weekly basis.

The spacious southern style porch with its old-fashioned wooden rocking chairs looked inviting, as did the elegant front parlor that was filled with clocks of all sorts. We counted three exquisite grandfather clocks that seemed to be keeping correct time and at least twenty old regulator clocks that had all begun to chime the hour as we entered.

The receptionist was an elderly woman with thick white hair and sparkling blue eyes. She was very pleasant and told us we could have a room with a double bed for $50. That included a full breakfast. We were overjoyed and booked the room immediately.

Later that evening as we snuggled in bed we recalled the highlights of the day and the past few months. It was hard to believe that just a short time ago, we were *strangers in the night* in every sense of the word.

I closed my eyes and thanked the fates for allowing our paths to cross, but the fates had some surprises in store for us that I could never imagine.

CHAPTER NINETEEN

Entropy

If you don't know where you're going, you might wind up somewhere else. Yogi Berra

AFTER A BRIEF jog in Prescott Park the following morning we ate our breakfast of scrambled eggs and toast in the inn's pristine dining room and then said goodbye to Portsmouth, heading north again in our yellow submarine.

We wanted to arrive in Maine by early afternoon, in time to visit rental places to see the summer houses still available. Gene was doing most of the driving, while I looked at maps and studied some guide books on New England, but when Gene told me he was getting a slight pain in his lower back, we exchanged places, and I began to drive. We rode along without any traffic for about another hour. Around two o'clock, it started to rain, so I stopped at a gas station and closed the canvas roof of the convertible.

Once we were back on the road, it had begun to rain more heavily. The winding, steep roads were growing slick, so I slowed down. I later learned that many roads in New England were beveled so they could allow the heavy snows of winter to drain faster. About twenty minutes after we left the gas station, it had begun to pour, and I was getting nervous driving along a wet curvy unfamiliar road.

I was just about to ask Gene if he could resume driving when in my rear view mirror, I saw a huge truck only inches away from us, flashing his lights and blowing his horn. I panicked and tried to slow down around the curves by downshifting from third to second gear, but as I did this, the gear stick jammed, and I did the worst possible thing a driver could do in that situation. I hit the brakes, went into a skid, flew over some gravel on the side of the road and then careened down a small cliff.

Gene, in the passenger seat, reached over and tried to protect me from going through the windshield. The seat behind him came crashing down on his neck as the car rolled over in tall grass at the bottom of the ditch. I managed to crawl out, but Gene was trapped inside.

I thought the car was going to catch fire, so I tried to get him free, but he told me in a calm voice to get help because he had a neck injury and he didn't want me to move him.

Fortunately, just then I heard voices behind me and when I turned around, I saw several young men scrambling down the hill to help. They were all speaking French, but there was no need to communicate because they saw the situation and knew what was happening.

Gene managed to let them know that his neck was injured by using a few French words and hand gestures. Very carefully they lifted him from the car and placed him on the ground.

We were waiting about twenty minutes when we heard whirling sirens from an approaching police car. The policeman was very nice and he did his best to keep me calm, while he wrote down a lot of information from our driver licenses, registration and insurance cards.

He told us that the local ambulance was not available and that another official vehicle would be arriving shortly to take us to the nearest hospital which was about eight miles away.

The official vehicle turned out to be a hearse used by the coroner to pick up dead bodies and deliver them to the funeral parlor. Gene managed to walk to it, but I could see he was in terrible pain.

We had to sit in the back of the hearse on a long large box which I suspected was a casket. I hoped it was empty. I held onto Gene to make sure his neck would not be jarred by all the sharp twists and turns we were experiencing.

Needless to say, it was a long, stressful, and bumpy ride, but thankfully we finally arrived at the hospital in one piece.

CHAPTER TWENTY

Heisenberg's Uncertainty Principle

It's tough to make predictions especially about the future. Yogi Berri

JACKMAN HOSPITAL WAS a tiny hospital more like a clinic in the woods. It contained only twelve beds for emergency treatment and it seemed to be run entirely by nuns.

Two nuns checked us into the emergency room and two more took Gene to the X-ray lab where they stood him up and handed him heavy weights to hold in each hand while they took pictures of his neck from various angles.

Poor Gene was really in pain, and I tried not to cry or become hysterical. I was angry with the nuns who seemed pretty indifferent to Gene's agony and the precarious nature of his injury.

When the X-ray session was thankfully over, Gene and I were led into another room that contained two armchairs, a small desk and two filing cabinets. Gene wanted a glass of water, but the nuns refused to allow it because they said they would have to get permission from the doctor.

I was really worried that Gene was going to pass out from pain. Fortunately, the doctor finally arrived. He was a short man with dark skin, a dark thin mustache, and very curly thick black hair. I assumed he was from India, but when he spoke, he sounded like he was from Texas.

"So how ya' feeling?" he asked, sitting down behind the desk. "Had a little spill on the road, I hear. Well, the good news is that you ain't dead. The bad news is that you have a broken neck."

The room began to sway, and I had to hold onto my chair to prevent myself from falling.

"Well, that ain't as terrible as it sounds. You fractured a vertebra in your neck, not the whole neck. If you broke the whole neck, you'd be dead, understand?"

Gene nodded.

"Anyways, we can't treat ya here. We got to get ya to the big hospital in Waterville where they got an operating room and good surgeons."

"You think I will need surgery?"

"Of course. A fractured vertebra is not going to get better by itself."

It was the longest night of my life. Waterville Hospital was about 40 miles away and there was no ambulance to take us there, so we were forced to take another ride in the undertaker's hearse.

This time, however, the doctor insisted that Gene wear a surgical collar to keep his neck from moving and causing more damage. He also advised Gene to lie on a stretcher, rather than sit up for the trip since the roads along the route were very curvy and bumpy and lying flat would prevent him from further whiplash. I was told to hold Gene's stretcher in place as firmly as possible to lessen the possibility that it would go flying back and forth with each treacherous turn of the road.

It wasn't an easy job. I had to hold both my feet against the stretcher for the entire trip while trying to sound relaxed and reassuring for Gene's sake, but sometimes no matter how hard I pushed, the stretcher would start to roll.

Gene was so brave that night all through the long and uncomfortable trip, and he never complained even after we arrived at the hospital and he had to undergo a series of grueling screening tests.

It was after midnight when we finally were admitted to a room on the neurology floor. As soon as Gene was safely in his bed, I raced to the nurses' station and asked where there was a phone. I wanted to call Mick and let him know what happened, hoping that he would be able to help somehow even though he was miles away.

Sure enough as soon as I reached him and told him that Gene had a broken neck and needed to be operated on, he told me that he would leave first thing in the morning for the train station.

I knew that he had never heard of Waterville, since he had never been to Maine, and I realized what a long difficult journey this would be for him. When I told him I really appreciated his coming to support us, he laughed.

"Baby Doll, you know I would do anything for you. It's no big deal. And besides, I like Gene. I want to be there for the two of you."

That was my father. I hung up the phone wondering how I lucked out with the two most important men in my life. One was an angel. The other was a saint.

In the morning we met Dr. Rodriquez, a neurosurgeon and chief of staff of neurology at Waterville. When he first entered Gene's room, I had no idea he was a doctor. In fact I thought he was a golfer who had mistakenly wandered into the hospital while searching for the golf course. He was wearing a complete golfer's outfit from plaid trousers to Tam O Shea cap. The only thing missing were the golf clubs.

Obviously, he had been on the course and returned to the hospital to examine Gene as an emergency case.

"I looked at all your tests and X-Rays and they indicate it is your ninth cervical vertebra which is fractured and in danger of nicking your spinal column which could result in serious paralysis," he related matter-of-factly. "Now you can agree to have this surgery even though it comes with some serious risks, or you can decide not to have surgery and opt to wear a support collar around your neck for the rest of your life, hoping that you do no further damage."

Poor Gene was very pale, and he grew even paler as the conversation continued.

"How risky is the surgery?"

"Well, I've done these surgeries in the past and almost all of them have gone well, but if there is considerable bleeding, or if the spinal column is cut by the removal of some bone fragments, paralysis may occur."

"But that may not happen, right, Doc?" Gene asked in a low voice.

"Right. And I don't expect any serious complications. As I said, I've done this surgery before, and I have been almost always successful.'

"Almost . . ."

"Two of my patients had very complicated compound fractures that were pressing on the spinal column. Fortunately, for you, yours is a relatively clean fracture."

He smiled at me, but my face was so frozen in fear I could not smile back.

"You don't have to make a decision immediately," he said, turning back to Gene. "Think about it, but just don't wait too long."

"No," Gene said, "I don't want to wait. My wife and I just got married, and I want to get better so we can resume a normal life as quickly as possible. I want the surgery."

"Good," the doctor agreed. "I'll set up a few more tests and book the O.R."

With that he turned on his white spiked golf shoes and walked out the door.

I sat on Gene's bed holding his hand and trying my best to be positive and confident while I waited anxiously for Mick to arrive so he could hold *my* hand.

It took Mick about thirteen hours to travel from home to the hospital. When he entered Gene's room about 3 p.m., he looked like a ghost, pale and tired, but he didn't complain and immediately began reassuring us that everything would be fine in a few days and that Gene would be jogging again in a few weeks.

"Once they fix up that bone, you'll be good as new."

We told him about the upcoming operation and what the doctor had said about the risks, but Mick just shrugged off the danger.

"Gene, pay no attention, buddy. I'm telling you, you'll be fine. Doctors always exaggerate. That's how they jack up their bill."

Gene laughed.

We listened to Mick's tale of how his black cat followed him all the way to the bus stop on Washington Street.

"The damn cat almost got onto the bus with me. Blackie, she follows me all over the place. I bet when I get home, she'll be by the front door howling to be fed."

Blackie was not waiting by the front door when Mick got home. He searched all over the neighborhood, but he never found Blackie again. The poor animal was either killed by a car, hurt, or stolen by someone.

Mick with his soft heart was very sad, but he tried not to show it and pretended it was no big deal. I felt responsible, but there was little I could do for Mick or poor Blackie.

Dr. Rodriquez returned after 6 p.m. to tell us that the operation would take place in two days. In the meantime, Gene would have to undergo a procedure called the *Neurological Halo*.

"What's that?" Gene asked.

"Well, we have to drill small holes into your skull and then insert cables that will support weights to keep your neck in place."

"You. . . you . . .are teasing, right, Doctor?"

"No, I'm afraid not. This is the standard treatment now for a vertebra injury."

"But. . . drilling into my skull? Won't it . . ."

"No, it won't hurt. You won't feel a thing while the procedure is taking place. You'll be sedated. You'll just hear a lot of loud drilling. At worst, you'll be a bit uncomfortable when you fully wake up. But this must be done to stabilize your spinal column."

Gene tried to put on a brave face, but we all seemed a little dazed by this new information.

"When will I get this procedure?" Gene asked.

"First thing in the morning. No eating after midnight. And oh, you need to take an enema tonight."

By the look on his face, I could tell Gene was embarrassed as well as afraid. Here he was with his new bride and father-in –law and he was about to have an enema in bed. How humiliating for everyone.

"Ah, don't worry about it," Mick said, once the doctor had gone. "Everybody has to go to the toilet once in a while. An enema is no big deal. It will probably make you feel better once you crap."

Gene nodded, but I knew how he felt. I hugged him and told him I loved him. He smiled and pulled me down so we could kiss.

"Two love birds," Mick said. "Wait till the bills come in. Then love flies out the window. But maybe not with you guys."

The next morning the medical team arrived about 8 a.m. to take Gene to the operating room.

Although the hospital was kind enough to provide comfortable recliner chairs for me and Mick in Gene's room, none of us managed to sleep.

We couldn't imagine what it would be like to have someone drill holes into your head when you were half awake. The neurological halo sounded like medieval torture.

Gene was brave when he waved goodbye to us, but I could tell from his eyes that he was frightened. I blew him a kiss and promised I would be waiting when he came back.

Mick tried to calm me by suggesting we go to the cafeteria for breakfast, but that was the last thing I wanted to do.

"At least let me get you a coffee? Or maybe an orange juice?"

"O.K." I said, "A coffee is fine."

He was about to leave when he stopped, and took something out of his pocket.

"Oh, I forgot to give you this," he said, handing me a small white envelop. "King Farouk wanted you to have this."

Inside was a pair of rosary beads, a holy picture of Saint Joseph, and a little note that read, "Even though he is an atheist, I will pray for him. Good Luck, Ma".

CHAPTER TWENTY-ONE

Black Holes and the Disappearance of Light

Half the battle is just showing up. Stephen Hawkings

AROUND NOON GENE returned with a large metal disk attached to his head. He was a bit groggy, but he was smiling and seemed O.K. The top of his head was completely shaved like a monk's and there were six round little holes circling the bald spot. Inside each hole was a thin rod that was connected to cables that supported six ten pound weights. Needless to say, Gene was not going anywhere for a while, and his neck was certainly not about to move around either.

I was so happy to see Gene again, I kissed him several times as gently as I could, and would not let go of his hands.

The next twenty-fours hours waiting for the actual operation were sheer hell. Gene didn't complain, but Mick and I knew he was extremely uncomfortable being pinned down and unable to move. The thought of becoming paralyzed must have terrified him, but he didn't talk about it because he didn't want me or Mick to get upset.

Being inside a hospital room with holes in your head was a weird way to spend part of a honeymoon, but as far as I was concerned I was seeing a side of my new husband that would make me love and admire him even more than before.

Mick tried to lure me into the cafeteria moments after they began wheeling Gene toward the operating room early the next morning. I was tearing up as I kissed Gene good-bye and did my best to reassure him that we would be jogging again in only a few weeks.

He nodded and said that he hoped we would be doing "even *nicer* things" than jogging in a few *days*. His nurses, overhearing him, all laughed as they pushed him down the hallway.

"He'll be fine," Mick said, putting his arm around my shoulder. "He's got a good sense of humor. That helps heal everything. Now let's go for a ham sandwich or something. It will help get your mind off the operation."

"Thanks, Mick, but I can't eat anything now, and I won't stop worrying until Gene is back with us. You go."

"Ah, I'm not hungry either. But we should do something to pass the time, or we'll both go crazy just sitting around looking at one another."

He was silent for a moment as he stared out the window.

"How about a game of poker?

"Poker?"

"Yeah, I carry around a deck of cards all the time. You never know when they'll come in handy. ***And I think this is certainly the time.***"

Three hours later Dr. Rodriquez returned in his green scrubs and told us that all had gone well and that Gene was in the recovery room slowly waking up from the anesthesia. He said Gene would need some physical therapy for a few weeks, but after that he would be pretty much back to normal.

I was so relieved I grabbed hold of the doctor's hand and nearly shook it off his arm.

"Hey, Baby Doll, take it easy," Mick said, "The doc here has to use that hand to operate again on other patients. You don't want to break it."

Dr. Rodriquez laughed and took back his hand.

"In a little while, you can go down to the recovery room and see Gene. He should be awake by then."

'Thanks again, doctor," I said. "You saved my husband's life."

He smiled.

"Enjoy your marriage. I hope it's a long and happy one."

Over the next few days Gene slowly got his strength back and was able to sit up and talk with us. He was really anxious to get his halo removed, and every time the nurse came in to check his blood pressure or take his temperature, he would inquire about Dr. Rodriquez.

"Where is he?" Gene asked. "On the golf course? I want to get this damn thing off my head. It itches"

When the doctor did eventually show up, he was wearing his golf shirt and slacks.

He gave Gene a quick examination and looked over his chart.

"I think you're ready to have your halo safely removed. Everything seems stable now."

"I've been ready for days," Gene said. "If this thing stays on any longer, those holes in my head will be permanent."

"Behave yourself," the doctor teased, "Or I'll drill a few more to keep you quiet."

Once Mick knew that Gene was on the mend, and that I would be fine, he decided to head back home. It wasn't easy for him sleeping in a lounge chair and worrying about how my mother was faring without him.

"King Farouk will be lost without me if I don't head back," he said, looking over the bus and train schedules. "I need to check on her."

Gene offered to rent a car so Mick could drive home directly, and I was surprised when my father agreed.

"Drive carefully," I said, as I kissed him goodbye and thanked him for all his help. "I don't know how I would have gotten through this without you."

"You would have been fine," Mick said. "But I was glad to help."

CHAPTER TWENTY-TWO

When Fission Meets Fusion

You can't blame gravity for falling in love. Einstein

MICK WAS GONE only a short time when Gene asked me to lock the door to the room.

"But what if the nurses want to come in?"

"They can wait. We can't. We waited long enough."

He winked and waved me over to the bed. Then he took my hand and pulled me down so he could embrace me.

"There's no lock on the door," I managed to say while we kissed and cuddled. "Anybody could walk in."

"We'll tell them this is what the doctor ordered."

"I'm sure it's good for our health."

"It's good for our soul."

"I love you, Gene. I'm so thankful you're well again."

"You're so lovely."

"And you're so handsome."

It's difficult making love to someone with a broken neck who has half a dozen holes in his head and is attached to ten pound weights. I was terrified that I would hurt him and yet neither of us wanted to stop. It reminded me of a joke Gene once told me about two people making passionate love on railroad tracks as a speeding train approached. Unlike the couple, the train at least had brakes.

For us the sheer relief and joy of being together again after so many days of uncertainty and fear was just too much to resist. I have no idea who came up with the expression, "being on cloud nine," but that is exactly where we were until nurse Cracket, as Gene named her, opened the door, saw what was going on, nearly dropped her tray of medicines and test tubes, and let out a cry that would have shattered the calm of Mount Olympus.

Startled, I leaped from the bed.

"What in God's name . . . ."

"That wasn't exactly in God's name," Gene panted. "But thanks to him, your timing was perfect."

"I will have to let your doctor know about this. It is most unbecoming in a hospital room."

She turned on her angry heels and stormed away down the hall.

Gene and I began to laugh.

"What do you think Dr. Rodriquez will say?" I asked.

"I should think he will be very happy that he did such a good job with his operation."

"You certainly are making a quick recovery."

"Well, I have an incentive. I'm married to the most beautiful, sexy, and wonderful woman in the whole wide world."

I was tempted to climb back into the bed, but I didn't want to take a chance that Dr. Rodriquez would come in.

Instead, I decided to walk to the café and buy us both a nice big glass of ice tea. I thought Gene would do a better job of explaining things to his doctor than I could.

When I walked passed the RN station, several of the younger nurses were smiling at me and one of them even gave me the high-five sign. The whole situation was such a break in their regular routine and provided so many laughs that I felt pleased I had done a good service.

Every day Gene continued to get stronger, and he actually enjoyed his daily physical therapy sessions with a young man named Eric who loved the song, *McArthur's Park.* Gene loved that song too, so most mornings they sang it together while Gene did his exercises.

When therapy ended Gene was looking forward to a walk outside the hospital but Nurse Cracket did not approve of it. She probably feared that we would wander off to the nearest motel and not return until midnight. Fortunately, Dr. Rodriquez overruled her and gave us permission.

Once in the sunlight, smelling the sweet fragrance of honeysuckle and lilac, Gene, always the rebel, insisted on exploring the neighborhood. We began walking toward the main street of Waterville where there were shops, coffee and tea houses, and small cafes.

We strolled along slowly but after about twenty minutes, we came upon an inviting outdoor cafe with small white tables and charming matching chairs.

I was glad to have Gene sit and rest and when the waiter came by, I asked for two large glasses of ice water.

"Let's have a sandwich and a beer," Gene suggested. "I'm really tired of that terrible hospital food and a nice cold beer would be heaven."

We ordered grilled cheese sandwiches and two bottle of Heinrich beer.

We were relaxed and enjoying ourselves, chatting between bites and watching the people go by. We talked about going home, and what we would do when we got back into the apartment. Timmy had been living with friends when he learned about the accident and so the place was empty and would probably need some airing and cleaning once we were settled.

Gene also wanted to begin teaching again, and I had to prepare for another semester of college.

We were pretty much wrapped up in our plans and daydreams when I spotted Nurse Cracket standing only a few feet away staring at us.

"Hello," I said, waving my greasy fingers.

"I cannot believe *you people*," she said, shaking her head in disapproval. "Have you been officially released from the hospital?"

"No," Gene said. "We were walking and got hungry. We needed some decent food instead of that hospital fare."

"Dr. Rodriquez will be very upset over this. You are his patient and he gave you permission to walk only on hospital grounds. How do you intend on getting back?"

"The same way we came. By foot."

"Do you realize that you have just had a major operation and are not well enough to walk such a distance?"

"Well, I am a little tired, but that is why we decided to stop for lunch. You wouldn't care to join us, would you?"

"No, thank you. You know, I will have to speak to Dr. Rodriquez about this. Your behavior is most unusual and the hospital is responsible for your health."

"You mean you're worried about a law suit?"

"It is the welfare of all our sick patients that we are concerned about."

"Well, I promise you, I'm fine. And thanks to Dr. Rodriquez I am almost as good as new, so I wouldn't worry, Nurse Cracket."

"My name is not CRACKET. It's Crosby."

"Sorry," Gene said, turning his attention back to his sandwich. "Now please excuse us. We better finish eating here if we want to get back soon. My bed awaits us."

She shook her head in frustration and then turned and left without another word.

Gene was tired when we arrived at the hospital's front lobby about an hour later. But he was proud to have walked that far and grateful that he was still so agile and capable. The young nurses at the RN station smiled and waved when we went by. I could tell by their expressions that they knew we had "broken the law" again, and I was sure they all wanted to know the juicy details."

When Dr. Rodriquez returned later that night to reexamine Gene, he was so pleased with Gene's progress and determination that he said Gene could go home in two days rather than spend another week in the hospital.

"I just want you to take it a bit easy at first," he warned. "No horse back riding, no sky diving and no wrestling with 200 pound gorillas. Other than that you'll be fine."

He shook Gene's hand and said he would return for two more quick visits before signing the release papers.

Gene was so happy he pulled me close and gave me a passionate kiss as soon as the door closed behind the doctor.

"Before we get carried away again, Romeo, I think I better call Mick and tell him what is happening. He'll want to know."

Mick said he would rent a car and drive up to get us.

"You'll be more comfortable and a lot safer that way than riding a bus or taking a train."

"But that's a really long trip for you," I said. "And then you'll have another long trip driving us back."

"Look, I need another break from King Farouk. She's driving me nuts again with her nagging and whining. A trip to Maine will be my mental therapy."

Once more I realized how blessed I was with a terrific father and husband. What more could a sane woman want?

CHAPTER TWENTY-THREE

E=mc2

If you can't explain it simply, you don't understand it well enough. Einstein

T HE TRIP HOME went a lot faster than we thought. Maybe that was because we talked and kidded almost non-stop the entire way.

Mick, who had never graduated high school, learned a lot about literature, writing, mythology, art, and music listening to Gene tell stories about his days as a writer, teacher and theater critic.

Gene never talked like a pedant. Instead, he discussed writers and books the way friends would over a few beers. He made so many writers come alive by talking about the times they lived in, their relationships with other writers, and their eccentricities and weird lifestyles.

"James Joyce was a literary genius, but he carried his wife's panties in his pocket and wrote her naughty letters filled with sexual terms that shocked his Irish Catholic community years later when they were discovered."

"After the recent scandals in the church, I think dirty letters to a woman written over a hundred years ago ain't too bad," Mick said as we drove along.

"Amy Lowell, a well known poet from New England, smoked cigars, dressed like a man, and liked to shock her brother, the president of Harvard, by sitting down in the gutter to read her poems aloud to passer-bys."

"Yeah, those poet types are a strange breed," Mick said. "Patti was telling me about that Welsh guy Dylan Thomas who drank like a fish and wound up killing himself by downing 18 straight shots of whiskey in the White Horse Tavern in New York."

"He was a gifted poet but a troubled man," I interjected.

"Why are so many writers so crazy?" Mick asked.

"Oh, there are many reasons," Gene replied. "Some of them are emotionally immature, some let celebrity go to their heads, some suffer from depression, and others have real mental illnesses."

"Then there are people like William Burroughs, who shot and killed his wife because he was high on drugs, and Norman Mailer, who stabbed his wife at a party because he was angry and drunk."

"And what about his relationship with Jack Abbot, the criminal whom Mailer helped get out of prison. Mailer sponsored his book, *The Belly of the Beast* and made the guy rich overnight."

"What happened to him?" Mick asked

"Abbot wound up killing a young waiter in a New York restaurant when the innocent waiter asked him to use a bathroom on the outside of the building because the one inside was being repaired."

"Jesus," Mick said. "Talk about an over reaction."

"Mailer tried to explain Abbot's action by saying that his years in prison conditioned him to believe that he was going to be sexually assaulted by the waiter. But neither the court nor the people accepted Mailer's explanation, and Abbot was found guilty of murder and sent back to prison for life."

"And what became of his book? Did he make money from it?"

"I believe the book's royalties went to the family of the murdered waiter. Abbot never saw a dime."

"Well, that was a good thing."

To pass the time, Gene told Mick about O'Henry, one writer he had heard of, whose literary career began while he was serving time in prison for bank robbery."

"Poets are especially high on the suicide list," I said. "Virginia Woolf killed herself by walking into the ocean with a raised umbrella, and Sylvia Plath stuck her head in an oven and turned on the gas during a terribly cold winter in London."

"Well, Gene," Mick said, after a long pause, "I'm sure glad you ain't nutty, even though you're a great writer. You got Patti Doll to look after."

"We look after one another," Gene said. "We're a team."

He stretched out his long legs in the back seat of the compact Italian Fiat that Mick had rented to save on gas.

"In mythology the gods often appear as bulls and horses and they mate with earthly women whom they desired."

I could see that Mick was beginning to blush, so I decided to change the subject.

"Our favorite writer is Albert Camus. He wrote a short novel called **The Stranger** about a man who kills another man and is condemned to death, but shows little emotion about anything except for pleasant memories he has of making love to a woman named Maria."

"He won the Nobel Prize but was tragically killed in an automobile accident when he was only in his forties."

Mick sat up straighter in his seat and gripped the steering wheel.

"Yes," he said, "When you're driving, you always have to be alert and careful."

"That's the irony," Gene continued. "He wasn't driving. His publisher friend was the driver. He insisted on taking Camus to his destination, even though Camus had already purchased train tickets and had them in his back pocket at the time of the accident.

Gallimard, the publisher, was speeding and lost control on a dangerous curve and slammed into a tree. They were both killed instantly."

"Well, at least he didn't know what hit him," Mick said. "That was a good thing."

"Camus often wrote about the absurdity of life. What could be more absurd than that, right, Mick?"

"Yeah, Gene. Who can ever figure out the mysteries of life?"

After driving for almost five hours, we all needed food, so we exited the highway and headed for a restaurant in Stamford that Gene always talked about.

It was called the **Monk's Place**, and although it had nothing to do with a church or religion, all the waiters wore monk's hoods and robes, and some of them even shaved their heads and had thick long beards.

Guests were serenaded with soft celestial music and occasional chanting, and on every wall there were tapestries of medieval scenes and portraits of saints and mystics.

Mick seemed a bit uncomfortable at first and even removed his baseball cap once inside the door, but after sitting down and joking with our young waiter, a handsome man who was probably gay, Mick began to relax.

"The biggest problem with this job is listening to people trying to confess their sins after a few martinis," the waiter said. "You would not believe the outrageous stories and shocking sins I have heard from the most normal looking people."

"Well, you can't always judge a book by its cover," Mick agreed. "Just because a man is wearing a nice expensive suit doesn't mean he's wearing clean underwear."

"Interesting," the waiter replied, "Now what can I bring you guys? You all look hungry."

We ordered the cheese and bacon quiche since Gene said it was delicious when he had it once before on another trip back from New England.

When the waiter returned, he was carrying a platter of apples and assorted cheese, a free treat that the restaurant was famous for.

Mick dug in. He loved cheese, especially blue cheese that he smeared on crackers and bread, but this was the first time he did it on apples, and he loved it. The poor man was so hungry and tired, I was happy to see him relaxed and eating.

Although I was very shaky to start driving again after the accident, I knew I had to. So after we left the restaurant, I drove the rest of the way to give Mick a much needed break. It wasn't easy being on the highway in so much traffic, but Gene and Mick had confidence in me, so after a few miles I settled in and calmed down.

CHAPTER TWENTY-FOUR

Newton's Law: What Goes Up, Must Come Down

The worst curse of being evil is that you can no longer experience the good. Michael Gruber

W E GOT HOME about eight p.m., and it was really a strange feeling to enter the apartment after so long an absence.

At first everything felt small and unfamiliar, but after living in a hospital room for several weeks, it was still good to be back and to sleep in one's own bed.

We wanted Mick to stay with us that night, but even though he was dead tired, he insisted on returning to see how my mother was doing.

No matter how much he complained about his King Farouk, it was obvious that he loved and cared for my mother. Like Gene, he was a loyal and decent man.

Over the next few weeks we resumed our normal lives. We returned to school for the start of the new semester, and although Gene had to take it slow since he was still mending, he managed to teach four literature classes three days a week.

I drove him to class every day and picked him up in the late afternoons. We usually headed home, had dinner, and then spend the rest of the evening reading, correcting papers, and preparing for the next day. I never imagined I could be so happy doing so many ordinary, routine tasks.

When things got a little too mundane, we would have a party. Gene always loved a good party with plenty of wine, good food, a marathon of story-telling and a riotous round of singing and dancing.

Everyone was invited: students, neighbors, friends, even people we just met. We held many parties over the years in our home, but the one that stands out so vividly is the one where Gene and I performed Tom Lehrer's *The Vatican Rag* to a houseful of our slightly inebriated guests.

We dressed as nuns in full uniform and with our black silk veils and long black rosary beads swinging in the wind, we kicked high our legs and danced around the room, belting out the hilarious lyrics to the loud, jazzy rhythms of Lehrer's lively piano.

> *First you get down on your knees,*
> *Fiddle with your rosary beads,*
> *Bow your head with great respect*
> *And genuflect, genuflect, genuflect*

People were literally falling off their chairs, laughing so hard as Gene, whirled around the living room in his nun's costume pantomiming the lyrics

> *Get in line in that processional*
> *Step into that small confessional*
> *There the guy who's got religion'll*
> *Tell you if your sin's original*
> *If it is try playin it safer,*
> *Drink the wine and chew the wafer.*
> *Two, four, six, eight*
> *Time to Transubstantiate.*

Years later people who were at that celebration told us they can still picture Gene singing his heart out and making everyone laugh.

On quieter evening we visited with Tom and Pam, our neighbors from downstairs. They would either come by for dinner, or invite us to join them in their apartment for drinks and conversation.

One night when we were in their living room chatting, Tom asked Gene if his neck was feeling any stronger. He wanted to know when Gene would be able to remove his neck brace.

"The doctor said I should wear it for at least another two months to prevent any sudden disturbance to my mending bones," Gene said. "I guess I can take it off around Christmas time."

"I don't want to rattle you guys," Tom replied, "but I think you should know what I heard recently from a good friend of mine, a cop here in this neighborhood."

"Apparently there has been a real jump in the crime rate, especially in muggings. He told me that criminals from Bergen Avenue are wandering onto this block and either breaking into apartments or jumping on folks they think are easy victims like old ladies and disabled people."

"Jumping on them?"

"That's right. They hide in trees and then when some poor sucker goes by, they literally jump from the tree, knock the person to the ground, and then rob him."

"Again, I don't want to scare you guys but that neck brace is a red flag. I'm worried for my wife when she comes home alone in the afternoons. My friend told me a woman down the block was mugged last week at two in the afternoon and wound up in the hospital with a broken leg. Some burly guy jumped on her, sent her sprawling, and then took off with her pocketbook and wallet."

As we listened, it suddenly dawned how unaware we were of the recent changes in Jersey City. Gene had grown up on Ege Avenue, a quiet block with middle class working families who believed in the American Dream and wanted the very best for their kids.

Now forty years later, a new generation of people had come into the city where unemployment, high energy costs, soaring rents, rising poverty and drugs were continuing problems. These stresses drove some people over the edge and led to crime and violence.

Living in our own safe, comfortable world, we didn't think about crime very much. We never imagined old ladies being mugged from trees. And we certainly could not imagine that we might become victims of this violence just because Gene wore a neck brace.

It seemed that the world and our own little slice of it had changed overnight.

After we left, Gene and I talked about what we could do.

We bounced around a few ideas like getting a big dog, or carrying mace, but every solution seemed to have its own brand of problems.

"If we got a dog, we would have to walk him every day and that would mean we would be out on the street more. And besides, right now since we're so busy, it wouldn't be fair to the dog to be inside all day."

"And if we got mace, which I think is illegal, we might wind up spraying ourselves in the face rather than the mugger."

"I guess we have to sleep on it," I suggested. "No sense panicking and acting rash over something that may never happen."

"True," Gene agreed, "but maybe we should consider moving and buying a house in a more rural area. Even if we are never mugged by the bad guys, it would be nice to have more space and to have a yard and garden where we could grow tomatoes and fresh vegetables. It would certainly be better for our health if we could breathe clean country air rather than bus exhaust."

It was the first time I discovered that my husband loved gardens and always wanted to have one of his own. I also was surprised to learn that the man who reviewed plays in New York City every week and liked exploring urban neighborhoods in Brooklyn and Greenwich Village, was considering rural living.

"But what about Timmy?" I asked. "Do you think he will like being away from Jersey City and all his friends?"

"Just because we won't be living here, doesn't mean we won't be here," Gene laughed. "I still have to teach and you still have to go to college, remember?"

"Does that mean we won't be moving to places like Pennsylvania or Vermont?

"Sweetheart, you have no idea how many beautiful places New Jersey has to offer. It's called the Garden State, don't forget."

"That's because of our famous Jersey tomatoes, right?

"Right. And besides the Jersey Shore, New Jersey has its share of mountains, lakes, and rich farmlands. Just a relatively short drive away from the city are dairy farms, horse fields, and little towns dotted with charming old homes and buildings."

"Sounds great, if you think we can handle it financially."

"Well, let's see what happens. We'll plan on a few trips and look at a few houses and see if any are good for us."

"O.K." I agreed, excited by the prospect of our new adventure.

CHAPTER TWENTY-FIVE

Manifesting

*Everything is accomplished by imagination
and persistence. Richard Feynman*

TWO WEEKS LATER on a Saturday afternoon in early October, we climbed into our Volkswagen bus and headed west toward Tewksbury, Lamington, and Long Valley.

We couldn't have picked a more delightful season to go house-hunting. Once we left the highway and began driving along the country roads of Hunterdon County, we opened the windows and took deep breaths of the cool fresh air, pungent with the scent of newly mowed grass and deeply packed mulch. The leaves were just beginning to turn their rich array of orange, yellow and red and every so often one leaf would drop in the soft wind and whirl downward before our eyes like a ballerina performing her final pirouette.

As Gene drove, I enjoyed looking at the countryside, occasionally catching a glimpse of several horses trotting around a lush green field enclosed by a white rail fence.

We passed several big red barns and giant silos stacked with hay. There were a few old dairy farms where black and white cows, chewing grass, stared at us as we sailed by.

Seeing the little town of Oldwick, part of Tewksbury Township, was certainly worth the trip. Along its main road there were several old Victorian homes painted in an assortment of tasteful colors to enhance their gingerbread effect.

We stopped at the Oldwick General Store to buy the local paper so we could check out any homes for sale in the neighborhood. The store was delightful with its sloping wide panel floors and massive chestnut beams.

We decided to have some tea and a piece of the freshly baked apple sauce raisin cake whose tempting warm sweet scent was irresistible.

Dried herbs and flowers hung from hooks in the ceiling and there were colorful ceramic bowls, mugs, cast iron pots, kettles, cauldrons and old-fashioned coffee pots on shelves throughout the place.

The paper listed four houses in the neighborhood. Two of them were older homes circa 1740 and 1784; the other two were newer built in the 50s'.

Fortunately, Gene and I had the same fondness for older homes, so we agreed to have a look at them. Both were being sold by the owner, so we didn't have to deal with a real estate agent.

We arrived at the first house after the owner, an elderly woman named Mrs. Barry, whom we spoke to on the telephone, gave us directions and told us to come by.

It was a small fieldstone house sitting close to the main road as many of the older homes usually did. It had a curving brick path leading to the front door which was painted a rich shade of blue, as were the shutters on the front four windows. Mrs. Barry opened the door and greeted us as soon as we rang the bell.

She was a sweet old woman with white hair and dancing blue eyes, and she seemed genuinely delighted to show us her charming home. We liked everything about it: the beamed ceilings, the wide oak floors, the narrow staircase leading to the upstairs bedroom and the old water well that was smack in the center of the living room.

It was so unusual to see a well inside a house that at first we did not believe it was real.

"Oh, it's real, all right," she laughed. I've been drinking from it for forty-five years, and it's the freshest tasting water I have ever had."

She pulled up a large stainless steel bucket from the dark belly of the well, fetched two glasses from the nearby kitchen, and offered us a drink.

The water was cold and sweet tasting and looked as clear and clean as water from a mountain stream.

"It's wonderful," Gene said, "But I'm still curious. Why did they build this house with the well inside? That certainly isn't typical."

"There's nothing about this home that is typical," Mrs. Barry said, proudly. "That's why I love it."

"If you love this house, Mrs. Barry, why do you want to sell it?"

"Oh, I'm not really selling it," she smiled. "You see, the paper offers free real estate ads to senior citizens every year for two weeks, and I thought I would take advantage of that and meet some nice people in the process. I get lonely from time to time, and it's so nice showing lovely people like you my beautiful home. It makes me so proud and happy when people like it."

We should have been disappointed and maybe a bit angry at being deceived, but we weren't. In fact, we were glad that Mrs. Barry was not going to sell her home. It seemed perfect for her, and just a bit too small for us, especially if Gene's children came to visit or stay. There was only one bedroom and one upstairs bathroom and the house was practically on the road. So we were glad we didn't have to mention these things to Mrs. Barry and possibly hurt her feelings.

Before we left, Mrs. Barry insisted we stay for tea and some of her home made scones. We had our little tea party in her charming kitchen which was small but very cozy like some English country cottage in Cotswold.

The second house we looked at that afternoon was only three miles away from Mrs. Barry's home. It too sat close to the main road and had no front lawn to speak of. The house was a little bigger than Mrs. Barry's, but it was made of wood instead of fieldstone and seemed badly in need of a good paint job.

It took some time before the owner, a man in his late sixties, opened the door and let us inside. He was the complete opposite of sweet Mrs. Barry. He said very little and kept looking us over as if we were about to attack him. He wore an old bathrobe that was stained with egg droppings and what appeared to be chocolate milk. The poor man smelled terribly, as did his home.

We knew there were cats on the property as soon as we walked up the broken front path since there was strong scent of cat urine coming from the nearby bushes and overgrown foliage.

We didn't wanted to spend a lot of time inside the house since we were certain we would never buy it, considering the condition it was in, but we felt we had to be polite and at least feign some interest.

It was difficult, however, to muster up much enthusiasm for rooms that were so cluttered and dirty. It was hard to believe that anyone could live there. It was a sad space for a sad man in an old bath robe.

The floors in every room were warped and stained with grime; the walls needed to be stripped of their ancient paper that reminded us of the hideous yellow wallpaper in Charlotte's Perkins famous short story, and every cabinet door in the musty kitchen was crooked and broken.

After making our painful way through the entire house with the owner following us, we headed for the front door as quickly as possible and said our thanks and good-byes.

On the way home we talked about how a house is the reflection of the lives within it, and how tragic it is when a beautiful home declines and becomes neglected, abandoned, and discarded in one brief lifetime.

"This happens to many people too," Gene said. "Life can be very difficult and unpredictable for many of us."

"No wonder the owner didn't want a real estate company involved," I mused, as we drove along the quiet roads now darkening with the shadows of twilight.

"He knew he would have to clean up the place and fix a few things."

"What do you think will happen to him?"

Gene was silent for a while.

"He'll probably die inside that house and his body won't be discovered until neighbors complain about the terrible odor. It's sad but that happens a lot to old people who live alone."

Neither of us said much for the rest of the trip home. We were lost in our thoughts, but I was grateful that Gene was beside me, and we were just beginning our lives together.

During my junior year in college I decided to minor in Philosophy. There were so many mysteries in life that I wanted answers to. What happened to people when they died? Did they just disappear into darkness or did their consciousness continue in some other form? Was the universe a random one where anything could happen or was there an order and harmony inherent in its nature? If people had free will and could make choices as the existentialists believed did that mean fate, and one's destiny were only illusions or linguistic misconceptions? Why did people fall in love? Was it just a weird chemical attraction or evidence of a soul connection that transcended time and space?

Since my life changed so quickly after meeting Gene, I spent a great deal of time pondering these questions. Marriage changed my name. Did my self-concept and identity also change? Who was the real me? The one Gene saw and loved, the one my parents knew and raised, or the one inside my head that never ceased talking. I realized I probably wouldn't find the answers I was seeking in a few philosophy courses, but I wanted to know what great thinkers like Heraclitus, Parmenides, Democritus and Plato thought.

After I found The Tao of Physics, a mind-blowing book by Fritjof Capra while browsing in a second hand bookstore in Brooklyn one afternoon, I longed to understand what Eastern philosophy had to say about reality.

Buddhism, Hinduism, Taoism, Confucianism, and Zen were all on my bucket list for study and thought.

It was hard for me to believe things just happen with no rhyme or reason. I hadn't planned on taking Gene's literature class. If the French class I had registered for had not been cancelled, I might have never met Gene. Was it chance or was I being guided in some magical way? If so, by whom or what?

Gene and I often talked about these questions over breakfast or while walking in the park. We never ran out of things to chat about and I think that was one of the reasons we never got bored with each other. He was smart and always funny. While I read books, he wrote them. His creativity was remarkable, and ideas for stories, poems and plays just kept coming.

Over the next few months we spent our weekends house hunting. There were plenty of houses available since the country was experiencing its first major oil crisis along with some big drops in the stock market and financial sector.

From a buyer's point of view, it was a good time to purchase since prices were falling and bargains were to be had. But interest rates were high and we needed to find a house with a mortgage we could afford.

Fortunately, the older homes that we preferred were less expensive and had much lower taxes than the newer homes. But the downside of these older homes was that many needed major repairs which could cost a lot of money.

We really liked some of the early Colonial and Cape Cod homes that we saw in Califon, a scenic and peaceful little town about ten miles west of Tewksbury, but they were all too far away from any major highway that would allow us to travel back and forth to Jersey City in reasonable time.

Route 78 had not been completed in 1972 and traffic on Route 22 East and West was heavy and slow. Some of the back roads were narrow and dangerous in snowy icy weather.

We tired quickly of the split level homes that had been built over the last decade on land that had once been thriving farmland.

One Sunday afternoon after seeing three houses that we did not like, we decided to visit a real estate office. It was after 4 p.m. when we saw the sign for Bergen Realty on Springfield Avenue in Berkeley Heights.

We thought that no one was there at first since the place was exceptionally quiet and dimly lit, but as soon as we entered, we heard a woman's voice from the rear of the room.

"Hello, there, folks. May I help you?"

We saw a short, very spry woman who looked about sixty-five, walking toward us.

"We know it's late in the day, but we were wondering if you know of any older homes around here that are for sale."

"Of course, yes, I can help you. Please have a seat. My name is Lee Cavelli, and I would be happy to show you some of our recent listings."

We introduced ourselves and described the house we were hoping to find.

"Well, if you like, I can show you a lovely older home that has been on the market for nearly a year now. The asking price is $80,000, but I'm sure the owner would be willing to accept a lower price at this time."

She leaned over the pile of papers on her cluttered desk and winked at us.

"The owner is a Mormon, and he is anxious to sell this home so he can move to Utah, where there is a large Mormon community in Salt Lake City, as you probably know."

"Why do you think it hasn't sold?" Gene asked. "Does it need a lot of work?"

"It needs some work, but you can take your time doing that. It is mostly cosmetic repairs and some minor remodeling, but the house has a large addition that is only ten years old and in excellent shape."

"Sounds pretty good," Gene said.

"Would you like me to call and see if the owner is willing to let us look at it now?"

"What do you think?" Gene asked.

"I'm excited," I said. "Let's give it a try."

It was only about three miles away, but unlike Berkeley Heights, Warren was sparsely populated in the early 70s and considered a rural community with dairy farms, lots of woodlands, and many homes built in the 1700s.

Lee drove us there in her big grey Oldsmobile, and chatted about the home's details and features.

"It was built by two brothers who served in the American Revolution. When they returned home, they purchased several acres of farmland in what is now known as Union Village. They built their house in 1784. Union Village is the oldest section of Warren and many of the houses date back to the late 1700s or early 1800s.

Right next door to the home was the former Union Village Methodist Church. When the church built a newer and larger building across the road in the 1950s, they rented the old church to a local theater group called the Stony Hill Players. They are still there and they perform wonderful plays and musicals four times a year."

"Do they accept original plays?" Gene asked, already picturing several of our most recent scripts being performed on stage by talented actors.

"Oh, that I do not know," Lee replied, "but you can certainly talk to Bob Meehan, the current artistic director who happens to be a good friend of mine. I'm sure he will fill you in on all the details. What I do know is that every performance I have seen was absolutely wonderful and very professional, especially the musical productions."

Gene was in heaven. He loved seeing and reviewing musicals, and he knew all the lyrics and melodies from most of the popular ones of the 40s, 50s, and 60s. He loved to serenade me with a tender love song or a lively show stopper from one of these shows.

"The house is no longer on acres of farmland since most of the property was divided and sold off through the years by various owners," Lee informed us, "but you still have over an acre in the backyard and almost half an acre in the front yard."

"That sounds like plenty of space for my garden," Gene laughed. "I want to grow tomatoes, zucchini, eggplant, peppers, string beans . . . ."

"You should have been a farmer," I teased him. "How do you ever expect to teach, write plays, novels and poems, take care of all the dogs we will have someday and still have time to garden?"

"I'll do that in my spare time when you and the dogs are sleeping and. . . .hey, what's this about dogs? Are we getting a dog soon?"

"What's a home in the country without a garden and a nice big dog," I teased. "Ever since I was a little kid watching Lassie every Sunday night on T.V, I always wanted a dog. Sandy was the only dog I ever had. Mick found him wandering the streets one cold winter day and brought him home. We loved him."

"What kind of dog would you get?" Lee asked

"Well," I said, "If we move into a nice big house with a nice big yard, then I think we should get a nice big dog. He would keep all the hungry deer from eating up Gene's garden."

"Well," Gene said, laughing, "Having a dog is great in many ways, but it can tie you down when you want to travel. However, I must confess I like dogs too, and I always wanted one. Unfortunately, the only dog I ever had was named Sputnik after the Russian spacecraft and poor Sputnik was killed when he wandered out of the house one afternoon. He was run over by a passing car. After that, I never wanted another dog."

I had never heard that story before, and I felt really bad for Gene knowing how sensitive he was.

Lee broke the mood when she announced we had arrived at the 1784 house.

"What do you think?" she asked.

I was not immediately impressed. The color was a sickly pale green, and the entire front of the house was blocked by trees and overgrown bushes. The path leading to the front door was grey concrete, broken in places with tufts of grass growing through the cracks.

Although the house was on Mountain Avenue, a county road, it was set higher up on a small hill with a fairly large front yard, so one got the impression it was far from the roadway.

Lee must have read my thoughts because she quickly assured us that the house could be painted, and the property fixed up without too much expense to give it more curb appeal.

"I'm sure you will love the inside, and wait until you see the country kitchen and the old farmhouse living room."

She rang the bell and after a few minutes, the owner, Mr. Kellogg, opened the door and greeted us.

He was a short, stocky man with a protruding stomach, light red hair, pale skin and very deep blue eyes. As he shook Gene's hand, I noticed that he had only one arm.

Mrs. Kellogg suddenly appeared beside her husband, wiping her hands in a pretty blue apron decorated with blue bunny rabbits. She was short too, and about twenty-five pounds overweight, but she had a warm smile and a lively manner, and as soon as we entered the home, she asked if we wanted to sample her blueberry muffins that had just come from the oven.

She must have known the best way to sell a house and impress potential buyers is to have something good baking in the oven when they arrive The delicious aroma of Mrs. Kellogg's muffins certainly had a positive effect on us, and as we walked from one room to the next we grew more intoxicated with the sweet scent of baking that was permeating the entire house.

Mrs. Kellogg proudly led us into her kitchen to sample her muffins. They sat on a large blue plate smack in the middle of a long farm table in the center of the room. It was a spacious room with a fireplace, a pantry, a breakfast nook, and a large bay window that overlooked the backyard and garden.

The floor was Mexican tile and shone with rich hues of orange and red from the glow of the pretty tiffany lamp that hung above the center table.

"This kitchen is so cozy and wonderful," I said, as Mrs. Kellogg handed me a muffin on a small plate. "It's just the way a country kitchen should be."

"Thank you. It served us well over the years. We cooked, baked, and ate many meals here. I hate to leave it."

She looked at her husband, clearly sending him a wordless message.

"Things change," he said. "We'll have another house in Utah that will be just as comfortable."

Mrs. Kellogg turned away and began fussing at the sink.

"Come into the living room," he said, leading the way.

The living room was just as magical as the kitchen. It was old world charm with its big stone fireplace and wide board floors, but it had an inviting, lived-in-look too, since there were kids' toys all over the floor and books and papers lying atop every piece of furniture.

A long hallway led to the library, bedroom, office and master bathroom in the new addition.

"I built this section myself," Mr. Kellogg said, taking us from room to room. "It wasn't easy with my one arm, but I saved a ton of money doing the work myself and doing it right. I used only the best materials for construction, electrical work and plumbing. Everything is in tip top shape, and you can rest assured this place will be standing solid a hundred years from now."

We were impressed, especially with the spacious bedroom and extra large bathroom.

"I designed this bathroom for my wife," Mr. Kellogg explained. "She grew up in a Newark tenement with a toilet in the hallway. When we were first married, I promised her that one day she would have a bathroom made for a queen. She loves it."

"I see you even have a bidet," Gene pointed out. "That not too common in America. Maybe France, but not America."

"Yes, Lee chimed in, "That so true. Not many Americans even know what a bidet is. One woman I was showing the house to thought it was a tub for washing her baby in. Her husband came to the rescue when he said it was for *washing her baby out*."

Gene and I laughed, but Mr. Kellogg seemed uncomfortable. He later confessed to Gene that he wanted the bidet for himself since he was allergic to toilet paper. It was an interesting fact that I could do without, but I found it funny anyway.

The library was a real treat for us. We did not expect to see a library with floor to ceiling bookshelves surrounding the entire room.

We tried to picture what the room would feel like filled with our books on a winter afternoon with the snow falling outside the window.

The only place that needed major repairs was the back porch. All the screens were torn and broken, and there was no real floor to speak of, just slabs of broken slate and patches of dull gravel.

There were four small bedrooms on the second floor and a large attic with a wooden trap door on the third level that was reached by climbing five short steps.

Gene joked that this was where a crazy uncle or nasty mother-in-law would reside, but Mr. Kellogg insisted that it was perfect for teenage boys whose loud music would not be heard by the rest of the household.

Lee began telling us another story about how she and two people became trapped in the attic after the hinge on the door caught on a nail and couldn't be opened.

"We were there until you arrived home at night. Do you remember that afternoon, Mr. Kellogg?" It wasn't too long ago."

"Oh, I remember all right. The people were so upset they never returned to look at the house again even though they seemed to really like it at first."

"I suppose that was my fault," Lee admitted, "But we were having such a wonderful time pretending we were little kids hiding from the world that I just didn't pay attention when I lowered that door."

I felt a little sorry for Lee. She was such a nice woman who was really trying to make everyone happy, but I suspected there was some tension between her and Mr. Kellogg.

Gene broke the mood when he asked to see the garden.

"Not much of a garden, I have to admit, since I never had time, but you can see there's plenty of space to make one."

We wandered out to the backyard and were impressed by the size of the property, but several of the trees looked badly in need of trimming, pruning and maybe even feeding. There was also a lot of debris around the yard, broken chairs, rusty tables, and plenty of weeds.

"The yard needs some tender loving care," Lee said, "But the property has a lot of potential and it's the largest lot in this area."

"I didn't have much time for yard work," Mr. Kellogg said, "And my boys didn't help either, but we had a good time here. I was a scout leader and my troop used to camp out sometimes and make bonfires to cook their suppers."

I didn't say anything, but after hearing about those bonfires I realized why the trees looked so bad. The heat and smoke from the fires probably dried up their leaves and burned the bark.

When we were back in the house Gene asked about the oil bill, the garbage fees, and the taxes. I was grateful that he was more experienced than I in buying a house. He had bought and sold one before when he was first married, and he knew exactly what to ask. I was more concerned with the way the rooms looked and how wonderful the kitchen smelled. Foolishly, I would have agreed to sign a contract immediately without knowing anything else.

"Well, the taxes are just under five thousand, and the oil bill depends upon how much oil you use. If you get yourself a cord of wood and work the fireplaces, you can get by pretty easily all winter on little oil.

It was obvious that we really liked the house, but since it was getting late, we told the Kelloggs that we had to leave and would get back to them again.

Mrs. Kellogg insisted on giving us a bag of her delicious muffins to take home.

Back in the real estate office, Gene informed Lee we would probably like to make an offer.

"Wonderful," she said. "Call me whenever you decide."

CHAPTER TWENTY-SIX

Mind and Molecular Structures

Believe It In and It Shall Appear. Neville Goddard

WE TALKED NON-STOP about the house for the next two days. It was just the kind of home we desired, but the price was more than we could afford, and there would be additional expenses for repairs and renovations.

"Why don't we offer them ten thousand less and see what happens," Gene said, as we jogged in Lincoln Park in the late afternoon."

"Sounds like a good idea" I said. "And don't forget, once I graduate, I'll be able to get a job teaching, and we will have more money coming in."

"Big things ahead," Gene joked. "Now let's call Lee."

The Kelloggs accepted our offer after we agreed to pay the closing costs.

After hearing the good news, we invited Lee to join us for dinner at Charlie Brown's, a local restaurant where we loved the cold shrimp platter and the well-stocked salad bar.

We were all in fine spirits that night. Lee had sold a house after a long dry spell, and Gene and I were elated that we were going to leave the city for a beautiful house in the country.

We were looking forward to going to Wagner's Dairy Farm where the milk was fresh every day and home made apple and blueberry pies were the specialty of the house. We were also glad to know that Wagner's farm actually delivered milk right to the door in glass bottles by a man in a white shirt and cap, just like the old days.

The only thing missing was his horse-drawn cart. Instead, he drove a small milk truck with the words *"**Wagner's Diary**"* painted across the side in blue, white and red letters.

A few years after we were settled in Warren, we almost bought that little milk truck when it was on sale outside the farm, but when we learned it had no heat we decided against it.

While celebrating at Charlie Brown's Lee told us a lot about herself. We learned that she had married a man named Gene who was also older than she. They had been married for nearly 45 years when their two sons surprised them with a cruise vacation for their upcoming wedding anniversary.

Lee told us how she and her husband celebrated like a king and queen for several glorious days, sailing along the Atlantic under blue open skies. She said she always enjoyed the smell of sea water, and each morning she and her husband would rise early and stroll along the upper deck, inhaling the fresh salty air and enjoying the mild warm breezes off the ocean.

"We were so happy," Lee said, sipping her small glass of brandy. "Then one morning it all came to an end the way everything comes to an end. My darling Gene told me he wasn't feeling too well as we took our morning stroll. He looked pale and he was breathing funny, so naturally I got really scared. I grabbed his arm and was about to take him to the infirmary when all of a sudden he collapsed. He went down like a ton of bricks, and when I looked at him there on the ground, I knew he was gone. It was the worst day of my life."

She fished into her handbag and took out her wallet. Inside were photos of them hugging and kissing like teenage lovers.

"It's been ten years now since Gene passed away, but it feels like only yesterday. I still miss him with all my heart."

We knew exactly how she felt, and we tried not to picture ourselves in that same awful scenario.

Gene tried to comfort Lee by reciting a few lines from his favorite poem by William Shakespeare, *That Time of Year.*

This thou perceiv'st, which makes thy love more strong,
To love that well which thou must leave ere long.

"My Gene loved poetry," she said, wiping away a tear. "That was so beautiful. He would have loved hearing it."

"It's sounds as if you had a wonderful marriage," I said. "You had those years together. How blessed you are with memories."

"Well, speaking of a wonderful marriage, it seems you two are heading in that direction. Buying a home together is just the beginning of so many wonderful times. I wish you both much luck and good fortune in the years to come."

"Our friendship with you, Lee, is just beginning. You certainly know where we live now, so please drop in whenever you like. You're always welcome."

"We are pretty lucky," I said. "Not only did we find a house, we found a new friend in the neighborhood too."

Mr. Kellogg was very kind to allow us to bring some furniture from time to time to store in his basement before we actually moved in.

My father, who was working part-time as a driver for the Appellio's Fish Market in Jersey City, said he would help us in our final move by borrowing the fish truck from his boss, a longtime friend.

The closing was set for April 13th, which gave Gene plenty of time to plan his garden and buy his seed.

It was a treat when we drove to the house, usually on a Sunday afternoon. Mrs Kellogg would be in the kitchen as usual, cooking or baking her delicious pies and muffins.

It was during these visits that we got to meet some of their kids who were anything but shy. They would run around the yard playing games and shouting at each other, or ride their bikes round and round the driveway singing songs, calling one another names, and performing dare-devil stunts on their bikes and skates for our attention.

"I wonder if the house will feel lonely when these kids are gone," I mused to Gene. "Unless your own children come and stay for a while, the house will have only us to keep it company."

"Well, it will be a lot quieter, that's for sure. I think the house might appreciate that."

It was on our second visit that Mr. Kellogg announced that he had something to show us that nobody had mentioned before about the house.

We thought it was going to be some problem with the furnace or the roof or maybe even the plumbing, but when Mr. Kellogg opened the back door to the yard, we knew it had nothing to do with the house itself.

We walked a short distance before noticing a small red and white structure hidden behind several large trees.

"I forgot to mention that we have a horse barn," Kellogg said. "It dates back to the 1800s. If you ever want to get a horse, you got the home for him right here."

We were so surprised, we ran past Mr. Kellogg and dashed into the barn. Never in our wildest dreams did we imagine ever owning anything like it. It was a small century old barn, as Mr. Kellogg described, but stepping inside was like entering another world.

The dark smoky wood and ancient floors still held the scent of hay and horse flesh, and the heavy oak beams on the ceiling silently told the story of days long gone and lives long forgotten. There were old oil lanterns hanging from the rafters and rusty iron tools for hammering, sawing, and sanding, scattered here and there on dusty shelves and corner nooks.

"I did some history of this house down at the county library, and I learned that the Coddington family had lived here in the early 1800s. They are a pretty famous family here in Somerset County. In fact, a lot of roads were named after them all through the state."

"Yes, I did see a Coddington Lane as we rode through the town one afternoon," Gene remarked. "So they lived in this house, you say?"

"Yes, and they are all buried in a small cemetery right here on Mountain Avenue, just about a half mile away."

"There's a cemetery here?" I asked, really surprised. "We didn't see it."

"Oh, it's back from the road and not marked. In fact, it's in a small lot between two houses and not many people know it's there. But if you walk back a bit you can see the headstones. They are all pretty old and broken now, but you can still read names and dates."

"We'll have to go and take a look," Gene announced. "That will be really interesting."

"One grave belongs to a baby of only six months and another grave belongs to her dad who died of a heart attack in this barn only three weeks after his baby died."

"Oh, God, that must have been so sad for the rest of the family, "I said.

I was beginning to realize how much energy and emotion our new home held from so many previous generations who had lived there.

"No need to worry," Mr. Kellogg said, perhaps reading my mind. "I've lived here for about twenty years now and I can assure you the house is not haunted."

"We felt only good vibrations when we entered your home," Gene replied. "In fact, that was one of the reasons we decided to buy this house. It's calming, comfortable, and warm in spirit."

"Yep" he agreed. "Especially when my wife is baking."

A few weeks later it was time for the closing, an especially exciting day for us when papers would be signed, and everything would become official, so we could finally receive the keys to our new home and move right in.

We felt sorry for Mrs. Kellogg who was crying over leaving behind so many good memories, but Mr. Kellogg seemed relieved to pile his family into their spacious RV and head for the hills of Utah where his Mormon friends were waiting to welcome him.

Mick as always was a godsend as he helped us moved furniture and boxes out of the apartment and into the house. He seemed to like the place and every now and then he would step out into the backyard and gaze up at the trees and sky.

"Those trees have seen a lot of life go by," he mused. "Imagine if they could talk? And just think—they will probably still be here long after we're dead and forgotten."

"Oh, Mick, you will never be forgotten," I said, hugging him, "You'll always be Mick, the Hoboken fireman, who drives a fish truck part time and loves his daughter, son, King Farouk, and his new son-in-law very much."

When Lee came for a visit, we learned about the old woman whose house was directly across the road from ours.

Her name was Lillian Conrad and when her husband died he left her in charge of his prosperous record company in Plainfield. She was as sharp as a whip but very eccentric. She lived with twenty cats inside her large house and after we got to know her better, she told us that her cats had gone a bit crazy when they smelled our fish truck, parked so close to their home.

"I thought you were going to open a fish market in the neighborhood when I saw it parked in your driveway. I had no idea you were using it as a moving van."

She also said she thought Mick was Mr Appellio, the fish man whose name was posted on the side of the truck.

"He didn't look Italian," she said. "So I was confused until you told me his name was Mick. Anyway, I like him. Does he like cats, by the way?"

CHAPTER TWENTY-SEVEN

Jumbo and the Law of Inertia

If Anything Can Go Wrong, It will. Murphy's Law

OUR MOVE WAS pretty successful. The only casualty was our very old and very heavy barber chair which we purchased at an estate sale in Newark two months before we bought the house. We had it in our apartment's bedroom, and Gene sat on it at night and read before going to bed.

It weighed about two hundred pounds since it was made of heavy metal and steel, but it was a gorgeous looking chair with a red leather seat and white marble arm rests.

Since it was way too heavy for Gene and Mick to carry, my father suggested that we hire a guy that he knew in the moving business named Jumbo who weighed over three hundred pounds and could lift almost that much weigh by himself.

It sounded like a good idea until we actually met Jumbo and saw how physically unfit he was. He was eating a greasy hamburger when he arrived to look at the barber chair, and although we tried to discourage him from taking on the job, he insisted that he could easily manage it and just wanted to know how far he would have to drive to deliver it.

"Our house is in Warren, New Jersey."

"Never heard of it," he said, swallowing the last bite of his burger. "How long will that take to drive to?"

"About 45 minutes," Gene said.

"Well, that sounds O.K. but I will need to stop for a snack along the way. I can't go that long without eating something."

"If we go along Route 22 there are plenty of diners to choose from."

"Great," Jumbo said. "In that case when do you want this thing moved?"

We were surprised when Jumbo showed up two days later with his buddies, two more fat guys who looked like they too were candidates for the cardiac ward in Overlook Hospital.

Gene, Mick and I watched in terror as all three struggled to lift the barber chair and carry it through the door of the apartment and down the stairs to their truck, a broken down Chevy with no exhaust pipe and a broken muffler.

They started to sweat as soon as they realized that all three of them and the large barber chair would not fit through the doorway. They tried shifting positions, turning the chair first to the right and then to the left and then slowly easing it to the floor while they racked their brains trying to figure out the best way to proceed.

When Gene suggested that they place a blanket under the chair and tip it on its side and then drag it out the doorway, all three seemed relieved to follow his instructions.

He also suggested that they use the elevator rather than carry it down the stairs. They agreed that was a great idea and slapped Gene on the back, declaring him one "hellava smart guy."

The only thing they didn't seem to like was when Gene cautioned them not to get on the elevator all together along with the chair since their combined weights would probably break it.

"Walking will do you boys some good," Mick teased. "You all look like you could lose a few pounds."

When they finally got the barber chair out of the building and into the truck, we thought all our worries had been for naught, but when we stopped on Route 22 because Jumbo announced that he was starving and had to eat something right away, or he would die, we suspected there was still danger ahead.

We waited in the truck while Jumbo and his friends ordered their take out.

"Let's hope that they're buying something light and nutritious," I said. "If they eat too much, they'll fall asleep carrying the chair."

After about twenty minutes all three returned, chowing down on double cheese burgers, French fries and giant slurpies.

Sailing along Route 22, with his burger in one hand and the steering wheel in the other, Jumbo was no poster child for safe driving, but fortunately we all arrived at the house in one piece.

There was a lot of grunting and burping as Jumbo and his pals tried to remove the barber chair from the back of the truck. Mick, Gene and I held our breath and silently prayed that no one would be hurt, but I suppose we didn't pray hard enough for the chair because just as it was being lifted in mid-air, Jumbo's fat legs began to totter, and he fell backwards, losing his grip and allowing our poor barber chair to crash to the pavement.

Everyone was O.K., but the chair's footstool was broken off and one armrest was badly dented.

"Nice going, Jumbo," Mick said, picking up the broken piece. "Remind me to write you up a good recommendation for future references."

After resting for a while, Jumbo was ready to bring the chair into the house by going through the backyard and putting it on the porch. There was no floor to worry about damaging, so it didn't matter that they dragged it almost all the way.

We paid Jumbo and his pals as quickly as possible, so they would leave as quickly as possible before Jumbo asked for supper.

We planned on staying in the house that night rather than risk another ride with them. We were hoping that Mick would stay too, but he said he wanted to check up on my mother.

"You guys have a relaxing night in your new home," he said, waving goodbye.

"If you see any ghosts, tell them you charge rent."

That evening we ordered a pizza and were eating it in the kitchen surrounded by a dozen unpacked boxes and stacks of books when the doorbell rang. At first we didn't know what the sound was since we had never heard it before, but when it chimed a second time we knew someone was at the front door.

It was Lee smiling happily and holding a small box.

"I came to bring you a housewarming present. In a house this size you cannot be without one of these."

She followed us into the kitchen where she handed me the box. I heard a low purr and felt the box move in my hands.

Inside was a tiny black kitten with a long white streak running across its button nose and chest.

"You can always use a good cat in a country home," Lee said, stroking the kitten's head. "It will eat mice, keep away rats, and warm your laps on cold winter nights."

Neither Gene nor I ever had a cat before and didn't know much about them, but this kitten was so adorable and tiny, we fell instantly in love.

"What do we feed her?" Gene asked. "I take it she's too young for pizza."

"Correct," Lee laughed, "But if you don't mind I would like a slice. I'm starving."

"This is a wonderful way to celebrate a new home," I said. "Friends, pizza pie and a new kitten."

"Just keep it warm tonight and give it a little milk and she'll be fine." Lee said, biting into her slice of pie.

"I hope we can still get a dog. A house is not a home without a dog."

"If you get a puppy, the puppy and kitten will grow up together and become the best of friends," Lee said. "Just don't get a full grown dog or you may have problems. But who knows? Some animals get along fine no matter what."

"Well, all we need next is a white picket fence," Gene teased. "Then we will be the All-American family: A white fence, a cat, a dog, and my kids running wild."

We named our kitten Camus, after Albert.

Beginning that night and for the rest of Camus's life, she slept in our bedroom, first in a little box during her kitten stage and then at the foot of our bed, the way dogs do.

I felt so safe and calm that first night in our big new home with Gene beside me in our new king size brass bed and Camus at my feet. Outside the windows I could hear the wind and the distant rumble of the New Jersey transit train in Berkeley Heights. It was a pleasant sound in the darkness, evoking images of middle age men in suits arriving in lonely train stations late at night. I thought of John Cheever and all the short stories he had written about such weary men on trains coming home to dull lives and dying marriages with only the solace of alcohol and illicit sex to comfort them and help them get through the night.

The next morning we woke to the soft crying of Camus wanting breakfast and hugs. It was a bright sunny morning and the kitchen was filled with an inviting light that made it a joy to prepare breakfast. Even though I am not a fan of coffee I love the smell of it brewing, so I made a pot along with a kettle of tea and some hot apple cider for later.

Most people say it is a hassle to move and it can be exhausting and frustrating, but moving into a big house was a pleasant experience for us. We enjoyed roaming from room to room and putting a few things here and there. We felt like we were truly making it our home as we arranged furniture and hung pictures and put books on the shelves in our new library.

Although Gene had lived in a house before with his ex-wife and children, this house had more rooms and twice the square footage, so it felt much bigger and more spacious than any place he had ever lived.

We planned on getting a piano and filling the living room with music for parties and celebrations. Gene was able to read some music, and he could pick out a few tunes, especially the old Broadway hits from musicals like **My Fair Lady**, **West Side Story**, and **Man with a Load of Mischief**, one of his favorites.

Having a beautiful piano in the living room would inspire us both to sing, write, and enjoy those special old-fashioned moments when the family gathered round the piano to celebrate their lives together.

One week after we moved in, Gene's youngest kids came for a visit.

Terry loved the backyard and spent more time climbing trees than he did playing in the house with Celine and Tara, who enjoyed their favorite game of hide and seek by getting lost in the most secretive spots in the house like the crawl space in the upstairs attic and the hidden closet beneath the staircase leading to the basement. We had a good time taking the kids for chocolate milk and apple pie down at Wagner's and it was a treat to watch them cuddle with the diary cows and feed the horses apple slices and carrots.

In a different way we were becoming a family, getting to know one another as individuals and learning slowly to adapt to change and the unexpected.

It was a nice feeling to know each child had a room and space of his own whenever he or she wanted to visit or stay, and that each one of them was growing more comfortable with me as a friend and big sister rather than a second "mother."

We saw the older kids, Chris, Colleen, Carolyn and Eugene less frequently, mainly because they were involved in their own worlds of school, work, and friends, but Gene did his best to always remain close and open when they needed him.

In the years to come as divorces became more common and the family unit shifted and evolved in ways no one would have dreamed of, children were better prepared when their parents separated and remarried. But back in the sixties and early seventies the stigma of a broken home often left many scars on children. That was why I was happy when Gene and his children tried their best to hold things together, and I was part of it.

CHAPTER TWENTY-EIGHT

Nature Abhors a Vacuum

If every time we observe, there is a new beginning, then the world is creative at the base level. Amit Goswami

SINCE WE HAD such a big house to fill with furniture and treasures, we began going to garage and estate sales over the weekends. It became an activity that we would enjoy for years to come. In fact, as the years went by, and we kept accumulating more stuff, we eventually ran out of space and had to purchase sheds from the Amish in Pennsylvania to neatly store all our books and goodies.

After forty-six years of garage-sale shopping, we wound up owning nine sheds, one large gazebo, and one big greenhouse for flowers and plants. Gene christened one of these shed's *Patricia's Tea Room* because he knew how much I love drinking tea and buying interesting tea pots for my collection. He created a white pebble path circling the yard and leading to every shed. Since the total effect resembled a little village, he called the backyard, *Flinns' Village.*

On Saturday mornings, Gene would get his road maps together, (this was years before GPS devices would become so popular), scan the classifieds for available sales, plan a route, and then gather together some cash from our piggy banks, so we could negotiate successfully with sellers.

It became a game in many ways and Gene was really good at it. We would see something we liked such as a fine original painting or a brand new kitchen gadget still in the box. Then we would look at the price tag and discuss what we might offer to get the best deal.

Some sellers were stubborn and refused to accept offers on anything. This really annoyed Gene, so we would always leave the sale before buying anything.

But if I really liked something, Gene would do his best to get it for me.

Eventually we got pretty good at the game. We learned that prices would always drop on a late Sunday afternoon, so that was the time we shopped for bargains.

One Sunday we bought an antique oak table with four matching oak chairs for just a hundred dollars. On another occasion we found a tiffany lamp for eighty-five dollars, but our best deal was when we walked away with a whole set of copper pots and pans for fifty dollars.

Sometimes we couldn't believe the outrageous prices people put on their things. We were in a home where a divorced woman was selling two Italian leather couches that would have cost about four thousand dollars new in stores. She was selling the two of them for only twenty bucks. We thought we were reading the sale tag incorrectly, but when Gene questioned her, she explained that they belonged to her ex-husband whom she was not very fond of. He insisted she sell them and give him the money. That afternoon we handed over twenty bucks and left with two great couches.

Our greatest bargain, however, was in Chatham. A woman, who was well known for running estate sales for wealthy clients, advertized that she was selling *"unusual treasures and rare pieces"* at her next sale.

We were excited. We liked wandering through unusual homes to see the odd ball things that people had collected over the years.

When we arrived in front of the house late Sunday afternoon, we didn't expect a crowd, but we were surprised when we entered the living room and there was no one there. Usually this was the room with the most activity. We wandered into the kitchen and again found the place empty. We eventually made our way through the rooms of the entire first floor and found no one.

"This is kind of creepy," Gene said. "I wonder if we should leave."

"Why don't we check upstairs," I said. "Maybe there's somebody in one of those rooms."

When we got to the top of the stairs, I could see there were several rooms with open doors to our right and left. We turned right and found ourselves in what looked like an office. There were filing cabinets across the entire back wall and smack in the center of the room was the most unusual and beautiful desk we had ever seen. It was huge and made of rich golden teakwood.

"This is one lovely piece of furniture," I said, reaching out and touching it.

Gene agreed and began looking for the price tag. We found it in the center drawer. $1,200 dollars.

"Way beyond our budget," I said. "But it's still a bargain. In a New York City antique shop this would probably be closer to three or four thousand."

"I wonder why it's still here," Gene asked. "It's strange it didn't sell. I would think dealers would have snapped this up first thing."

"I don't think they sold much," I said, looking around. "There's still a lot of stuff in the house and no one is here to buy or sell it."

Just then we heard a scream from outside the house. It seemed to come from the backyard and we went to a nearby window to look.

We saw a man outstretched on the grass, his arms above his head, his legs crossed at the ankles. It was the same position as Jesus upon the cross. He was shaking his head from side to side while moaning, crying and praying at the same time.

Beside him was an older woman who was carrying a tin box. She seemed distraught as she tried to quiet and comfort the man in the grass.

"What should we do?" I asked. "Should we try to help?"

"Yes," Gene agreed. "Let's go."

We dashed down the stairs and headed for the back yard.

"Excuse us," Gene shouted to the woman. "Do you need help?"

The woman turned quickly, surprised. She hurried toward us.

"Are you here for the sale?"

"Well, yes, but . . ."

Her question seemed so odd, I didn't really know how to respond.

"Yes," Gene answered. "But we heard this man in distress and thought you might need some help."

The woman waved us inside, clutching her tin box.

Once we were all in the kitchen, she shut the door, so we could no longer hear the man moaning and crying.

"Did you see anything you want to buy?" she asked.

"Buy?" I repeated. "What about that man? Shouldn't we do something?"

"Honey, that man is crazy. He's been acting like this all day. He scared away all my customers. Even the dealers were afraid of him. He's as nutty as a fruitcake."

"Who is he," Gene asked

"He's the homeowner. I should never have accepted this job. I suspected he was off his rocker from the very first time I met him. I just thought he would be with his sister on sales day and I could clear out this house before he returned. Now is there anything you would like to make an offer on? I just need to sell something and then get the hell out of here."

"Well, we did like that unusual desk upstairs in the office, but it's too expensive for our budget."

"The one for $1200?"

"That's right."

"You know that was a former harpsichord."

"Really? That explains the wonderful carved legs."

"The musical center was removed and drawers were crafted to fit it."

"It's really unusual."

"So," she sighed after a moment. "Make me an offer."

"Oh, I'm afraid we can't even come close."

"Look, you kids don't understand. This is not my stuff. It belongs to that crackpot who thinks he is Jesus Christ in the desert being stripped of his earthly goods so he can fit through the needle of heaven or something like that. I haven't sold a blessed thing today because of him. I just want to leave with something. How about a hundred twenty bucks?"

Our heads were spinning

"You would take a hundred and twenty dollars for that beautiful desk?" Gene asked.

"If you've got the cash, you've got the desk."

Gene quickly pulled out his wallet and handed over two fifty dollar bills and a twenty.

"Won't that man be unhappy when he finds out what you sold his desk for?" I asked.

"Honey," she said. "He's in left field almost all the time. And besides, what's the big deal? The price was 1200. I'll tell him I just left off one of the zeros."

"Can we have a receipt?" Gene asked.

"Here you are," she said, scribbling *sold* on a small piece of yellow paper marked ***Desk, $120. Paid in full.***

"You have to arrange to pick it up," she said, as she pocketed the cash.

"Once I'm out of here, I never want to see this place or that man again. So good luck and enjoy your new treasure. It's a real steal."

We didn't want to have Jumbo involved again in another move, not only because we were afraid he would drop our gorgeous desk the way he dropped the barber chair, but because we didn't want to have endless trips to diners and fast food places to fill Jumbo's bottomless pit of a stomach.

Instead, we hired a moving crew that was known as ***College Hunks for Service.*** Two guys who looked like they played on the NFL showed up in a white box truck at our front door about noon the following day. They introduced themselves as John and Joe, but it was hard to keep track of who was John and who was Joe, since they looked so much alike and wore the same outfit of blue denim shirt and jeans. They were polite and quiet and unlike Jumbo seemed in excellent physical shape.

We drove them to the house in Chatham and knocked on the front door, unsure of what to expect. A small thin woman with a pair of rosary beads in her bony hands opened the door and immediately asked if we had come to pick up the desk.

We handed her the receipt and introduced ourselves, pointing out that John and Joe were our moving men.

"What big men you are," she smiled, gazing up at them. "God bless you. I wish my dear brother was strong like you both. Instead, he is very frail, both physically and mentally. That is why I came here to help him today. I've been praying, you see, that all goes well."

"Yes, well, thank you. I'm sure it will."

John and Joe seemed anxious to get a move on, so I asked if we could start.

"Oh, yes. My dear brother has just taken his four tranquilizers so I'm sure he will be asleep by now."

She turned and led us upstairs to the room with the desk.

"Try to be quiet," she whispered. "Jacob is a light sleeper."

Joe and John took one look at the desk and announced that it was enormous, and that the job would not be as easy as they thought.

"Do your best," Gene said. "I'll up your fee if there's no damage."

The two linebackers positioned themselves at each end, counted to three and then lifted the desk off the floor. They tried to angle it out of the doorway several different ways but had no luck. It just would not fit.

"I wonder how they got it in here," John or maybe Joe asked, scratching his head.

"Oh, the legs come off," the old woman said. "I thought you knew that."

They were already sweating heavily from their futile efforts, but they managed to hold their tongues rather than insult the old lady for not telling them that sooner.

After a few minutes of rest, they lined up again on both sides of the desk, counted to three and then lifted and set it back down on its side so they could unscrew the legs. It took some effort, but they managed to get all four legs off. Now it was just a matter of lifting the table top, walking it through the door and down the steps into their truck.

Everything was going smoothly. They were halfway down the stairs when suddenly the crazy man appeared from the bedroom in his orange and white pajamas, shouting that there were robbers in the house, and he would have to get his gun and shoot them.

Joe and John, terrified, almost dropped the desk, but they managed to get it down safely and into the truck. By this time, Gene and I were carrying down the legs as fast as we could, while the old lady attempted to sooth her brother by saying a few Hail Marys from her rosary beads.

Safely inside the truck, we congratulated each other on a job well done and silently thanked the old lady for her prayers and rosary beads.

That night Gene and I sat in our chairs sipping wine and admiring our beautiful new treasure which John and Joe safely deposited in our library surrounded by shelves of books and some colorful paintings that we had bought at other estate sales.

Camus lay atop the desk purring contentedly and gazing back at us with her lovely green mysterious eyes.

All in all it was a very successful day. We paid $120 for the desk, $200 for the move, and another $50 for a tip to John and Joe who were exhausted but satisfied.

When Mick and my mother came to visit, they both thought the desk was wonderful.

"You can do a lot of writing on that thing," Mick said, patting Gene on the back. "It's big enough to hold at least a hundred books."

"Make sure you keep it dusted," my mother said. "And make sure you use Pledge polish. That's what I use."

CHAPTER TWENTY-NINE

Believing is Seeing

Reason is our soul's left hand, faith her right. John Donne

WE WERE LIVING in our house for several months when we heard voices coming from the playhouse next door. It had been quiet and empty because there were no productions during that time. But when we heard several people talking and laughing outside the theater, we thought it was a good opportunity to meet our thespian neighbors.

Bill Fleming was the artistic director; Norman Brown was the sound engineer, and Tom Edwards was the set designer and overall handyman. They were removing boxes and props from their cars and carting them into the theater when we arrived. They seemed surprised at first to see us, but when we explained that we had just purchased the house next door, they greeted us warmly, shaking our hands and inviting us into the building.

It was a wonderful space, just perfect for a small community theater. The ceilings were high, which was great for sound and acoustics, the front stage was visible from every angle; there was a upstairs loft where the lighting booth and sound equipment were, and the audience space was intimate and comfortable.

The old building was in great shape and obviously well maintained over the years. The floors were clean and shiny, the walls freshly painted, and the brass chandeliers over the main room were elegant and practical.

Bill, Norman and Tom took us on a tour, pointing out the costume and dressing rooms, the backstage, the prop room and several hidden spaces for actors to hang out as they waited for their cues or rehearsed their lines with the stage manager. It was obvious they were very proud of the theater and really enjoyed their jobs there.

Norman seemed to be the oldest of the trio. He told us he worked full time for Bell Labs as an electrical engineer, but would be retiring in a year. He also said he was looking forward to spending more time in the theater because he found it challenging setting up lights and sound for all the different productions.

Tom appeared to be in his mid thirties. He was tall and lean, but it was clear he enjoyed physical work like building sets and moving heavy furniture and props. His arms were thick and muscular, and he walked with obvious confidence and grace.

Bill had red hair and a thick red beard which was trimmed close to his face. He wore glasses and seemed more reserved than Tom and Norman. He gave us the impression of someone who liked to read, talk philosophy in a coffee house or café, and in his spare time direct plays.

They all seemed relieved when we told them we too loved the theater and were happy to have one next door. They confessed that they were concerned at first when they learned our house was on the market.

"Many people object to having a playhouse in the neighborhood. They think it attracts the wrong kind of people."

We all laughed. Gene said people have been thinking that way about actors for generations.

"Women especially were criticized for going on the stage. They were looked upon as fallen or wayward women, certainly not proper ladies."

"Are you interested in acting, directing, or what?" Bill asked. "What exactly would you like to do?"

"Well, we like to write plays and we enjoying acting too, so I guess we want to be involved in several ways," Gene replied.

"What kind of plays do you write?"

"Comedies, mainly, but also a few serious ones. Actually, we just started a play based on the life of Sean O'Casey, the Irish playwright."

"Really?" Bill said. "We performed his *Juno and the Paycock* two winters ago. It was a good production."

"We don't usually accept original plays," Norman said, looking over at Bill, "But I suspect there might be exceptions to that rule given the right play and circumstances."

"I'll drop something off, so you can take a look and see if it's right for you."

Back home Gene asked me what I thought about our conversation with Bill, Norman and Tom.

"Sounds like there are big things ahead," I said.

"I hope so," he replied. "But let's see what happens."

The next few months were very busy. While I spent time in the library studying for all my classes, Gene was preparing lectures and discussions for his classes. He was also teaching as an adjunct professor of theater at Rutgers. We worked on the house in our spare time, sanding the floors, painting a few rooms, and doing our best to get the yard and garden in shape.

The nicest part was being together. Except for when we were in school, we spent almost all our time together.

As a child, I was alone a lot, even thought I had an older brother, but after marrying Gene I was never alone again. Our friends called us the **Flinn Twins** and the **Dynamic Duo**. Whenever people saw me, they saw Gene and visa versa. For some reason we didn't believe that absence makes the heart grow fonder. For us, absence meant being lonely and sad.

Gene used to worry that I was safe even when I went to the post office, a short trip away. I was always concerned when he became sick with a cold or a stomach problem.

It was the only time I worried about the differences in our age. I couldn't imagine life without Gene. It was my greatest fear, and we always tried to avoid talking about it.

For the most part, however, Gene was an exceptionally healthy and active man. He ran, swam, and stopped smoking years before he met me. When we were dating, I knew he liked his martinis, beer, and brandy, but when he began having some bad hangovers, he gave up drinking entirely. He told me he did it for me and I believed him.

But every now and then he would come down with a serious flu or pneumonia that would put him in the hospital for a few days and leave him weak and exhausted.

Fortunately, he had great healing abilities which helped him recover so well from his broken neck. I called him my bionic man because he seemed so strong with so much will power and determination. Although I trusted that he would always overcome any problem that he encountered, I was devastated when he was diagnosed with leukemia five years after we were married. At the time I thought leukemia was a death sentence.

We found an excellent oncologist who informed us that there were several different types of leukemia, some very bad and some chronic and benign. Gene's was chronic and the doctor happily predicted that since Gene was in the zero stage, he might not need any treatment for twenty years or so.

"You have a long life ahead of you, Mr. Flinn," the doctor smiled. "Make the best of it."

We left the medical building that afternoon, a snowy one in January, feeling like it was a Spring day, and we had just won the million dollar lottery.

A few years later Gene felt a lump on his left chest when he was showering. We were overwhelmed when doctors told us it might be cancer, but after a biopsy, we learned it was a benign cyst. Even so, he left the hospital minus one breast nipple. I called him my Amazon man, after the women in mythology who cut off a breast so they could become stronger and more powerful in battle.

I think the medical diagnosis that troubled Gene the most, however, was when he was told he had macular degeneration. He was terrified of going blind. This fear was deeply rooted. He lost an eye when he was a teenager after he was shot with a staple gun fired by the neighborhood bully. Since it was his good eye that had the wet macular, Gene was understandably upset. For several months he had to undergo many tests and suffer painful shots directly into his retina. Eventually to our great relief his eye began to stabilize.

Like many people who go through a crisis and come out alive, we were determined to make every day special.

Gene was thankful for his children, for me, and for having Mick in his life. Even when he had problems with his eye and had to wear a black patch, Mick would make him laugh by saying he looked like a pirate in an old Errol Flynn film, or one of the bad guys in a Western starring John Wayne. They were best buddies in every way.

We were also happy to have Camus the Cat as part of our family since she made us laugh so much and brought so much affection into our lives.

Cats have a reputation for being aloof and not as affectionate as dogs, but Camus was not this kind of cat. She followed us around the house purring and rubbing herself against our legs, and when we sat on the couch she would jump up and park her hind legs on my lap and her tiny face on Gene's lap. She loved to be petted and stroked like a dog, and when we talked to her she would lift her head and gaze into our eyes with utmost attention. Neither of us ever had a cat before, and we surprised and delighted that she was so loving and adorable.

One day when we sat on the floor playing with her, I asked Gene how he felt about getting her a playmate.

"You mean get another kitten?"

"Actually, I was thinking about a puppy."

"Puppies need a lot more attention than kittens," Gene said. "But since you always wanted a dog once we had a house, I guess it might be a good idea."

"Oh, I was hoping you would feel that way."

"Should we get a dog from a shelter or just check the newspapers."

"I think a shelter is the safest way to go. We can check out the one in Somerville tomorrow and see what they have."

"O.K," Gene said. "But please control yourself when we get there. Once you see those poor dogs, you'll want to take them all home."

Gene was right. It was hard to walk past so many cages of dogs looking back at us with their sad eyes and drooping tails and not want to comfort and rescue them. A shelter is a safe place for homeless animals, but it is also a forlorn place with its long rows of metal cages, its cold cinder block walls, and its antiseptic smells.

As soon as we entered we asked if there were any puppies available. The woman in charge, an attractive lady named Wendy with large expressive eyes and a kind manner, told us the youngest dog she had was six months old.

"He was one of a litter of five from a homeless stray. A nice woman found the pregnant dog wandering around looking for food. She took it here, and eight weeks later came back and adopted the bitch and one of her puppies. The other three were adopted a few weeks later."

"Why do you think this dog wasn't adopted too?" I asked.

"Who knows?" Wendy shrugged. "He's a very sweet dog and loves people, but for some reason he just didn't go. Maybe he was waiting for you."

She smiled and led us down the hallway to where the dogs were kept.

When they heard us, they all began barking. In the middle of the room, she stopped and pointed to a cage.

"There's your guy. See. He likes you already."

Our guy, as she called him, was standing on his hind legs, leaning against the door of his cage, wagging his tail with such fury we thought it would fly off.

He was definitely a cute little fellow of mixed breed. He seemed a combination of German Shepherd and yellow lab, and although he was not too big, we could tell from the size of his paws that he would get much bigger.

Wendy opened the cage, and he flew out directly toward Gene, who was kneeling down to greet him. I could tell it was love at first sight. Gene was laughing and having a great time petting and jostling with him. The dog's tail was going a million miles an hour and his pink tongue was licking Gene's face nonstop.

I got on the ground too and joined in the fun. He jumped happily between us.

"What do you think?" I asked Gene, already knowing the answer.

"I think we should call him Chekhov."

"O.K. Anton Chekhov is his name. In honor of a great playwright."

Wendy advised us to introduce Chekhov and Camus gradually so they could get used to each other in stages. Although Camus was a hardy little thing, she was only eight pounds and very tiny compared to Chekhov who was already five times her size. If he greeted her with the same enthusiasm that he showed to us, Chekhov would flatten poor Camus like a pancake.

Neither of us had ever heard of crate training, but after listening to Wendy explain all the advantages, we headed to the local pet store to buy a crate that would comfortably house our new dog.

With Chekhov in tow on the leash we had borrowed from the shelter, we were one big happy family roaming the aisles of Pet Smart for things to buy.

Along with the crate we bought dog food, dog treats, brushes, bowls, a new collar and leash, name tags, and a few toys to keep him happy and busy.

We thought Chekhov might be rattled visiting a big noisy store since he had never been outside the shelter, but he quickly adjusted to the new sights and sounds by trusting and following us closely.

The sales clerk showed us a few different styles of crates, but suggested that we buy one that we could still use when Chekhov was a full grown dog.

"Just because he's small now doesn't mean he will be this size a month from now. He has big paws, so I know he will be a big dog and that means a big crate."

The crate was in a flat box so we were able to fit it into the back seat of the yellow submarine. The bad news was that we would have to assemble it.

We thought we were going to use the crate as a way of safely introducing Camus to her new doggy brother, but since that plan would not work now, we decided that Gene would hold Chekhov on the leash while I held Camus in my arms. Then we both would step closer and closer until both animals had a chance to smell each other and rub noses, so to speak.

I could hear Camus meowing as I opened the front door and called to her. Like a good little cat she came running toward me, but when she caught a glimpse of Chekhov, who was by then barking his head off and wagging his tail like a madman waving a flag, Camus froze, the hair on her back stood up straight and her spine curved upward in frozen fear.

There was no question Chekhov wanted to run and play, but it was also clear that Camus wanted to run and hide. From our perspective it did not look like "love at first sight."

It's hard to remember all the events of that night since so many things seemed to have happened at once, but the evening was definitely not a peaceful or quiet one.

We put the crate together, fed Chekhov his first meal at home, searched after Camus who was hiding in one of our bookcases, and tried to reassure each other that we had done the right thing.

Meanwhile, Chekhov was exploring his new home, smelling the furniture and running through all the rooms.

It worked out well that Chekhov and Camus never met face to face that night, despite all our planning. Instead they got to know each other gradually.

It took some time, but eventually it must have dawned on Camus that Chekhov was not going to eat her and that if she stood her ground, she would show him who was boss.

She did this by always being in a place that Chekhov couldn't reach. If he were on the floor, she would climb onto a high shelf and stare down at him. He would bark, and wag his tail. Sometimes he would jump onto furniture to try and reach her, but Camus was always quick enough to get away. They played this game of tag for a long time and seemed to enjoy themselves.

The crate was also a big help. Chekhov slept and ate inside it, and it became his second home, a place of security. When it was hard to keep an eye on him, we put him inside, knowing he would be safe and free from trouble.

Even though we had a big backyard, we still had to walk him on the leash when it was his time to go. Usually this happened shortly after he ate, but sometimes we had to take him outside several times and for longer periods before he did his business. Camus would be watching from the window, feeling infinitely superior because she never had to wear a collar or get walked on a chain.

We had Chekhov for over a month when Gene suggested we buy a fence so Chekhov could run free and still be safe.

"That will be expensive," I said.

I was turning into the practical one in the relationship. Gene always acted from his heart and did what he believed would make life better.

"Well, I think it will be worth it. And besides it will give us more privacy. Overall, I think it's a good investment."

"O.K" I agreed. "I'll call around and get some estimates this week."

It wasn't cheap but our new fence definitely was an improvement. I had shopped around and found a fence store in Chatham and within a week a crew of four men arrived and began installing it around the entire property.

CHAPTER THIRTY

Going Nuclear

If you judge a fish by its ability to climb a tree, it will live its whole life believing that it is stupid. Einstein

WE LIVED IN the section of Warren known as Stony Hill, and the name accurately reflected the nature of the soil and the difficulty of trying to dig anything in its dirt. The fence men grunted and groaned and complained to me every time I went out to bring them drinks and refreshments.

They implied by their surly looks and comments that Gene and I were responsible for the quality of the dirt. I could understand their discomfit as they struggled with rocks and stones and the heavy fence posts, but after a while I thought they were being unreasonable.

"If you don't want to work, quit" I said, after one of the guys threw down his post digger and cursed, as I approached with a pitcher of ice tea and a plate of ham and cheese sandwiches.

I am easy-going most of the time, but once I get angry, I find it difficult to control myself. I was born a Taurus, and like the bull, I will sometimes charge when I see red.

Although I often felt ashamed after losing my temper, Gene never criticized me. Instead he teased, calling me the **Terrible Temper Mr. Bang** from the comic strips.

Sometimes he would call me his **Powerful Katrina,** another one of his favorite comic strip characters who was exceptionally strong but had a bad temper.

Then he would kiss and hug me. I always calmed down after that. Gene had the magic touch for me.

Although Gene was gentle and slow to anger, when he did get riled up, he would brood for a long time. He was the opposite of me in that respect. I would forget the insult after a short time. Gene would hold onto it for a long time.

We managed to shrug off the dirty looks and unpleasant remarks of the men installing our fence when we saw how attractive it looked.

When I was a child I enjoyed watching Westerns like the **Lone Ranger** and **Bonanza** on T.V. Cowboys roped their horses to three rail fences and tough outlaws wearing black hats sat on these fences, smoking and playing with their guns. Fences were always an important part of a good Western.

I wished that one day I too would own a fence. Now twenty years later I was seeing my fantasy come true as I saw section by section going up.

I didn't have a horse and I probably wouldn't be sitting on top of our fence in a black cowboy hat any time soon, but I felt good that Chekhov could run free like a horse and enjoy his big backyard.

It took two days but our surly friends finished the job well. When all the posts and rails were in, they stapled heavy green wire over every section so the rails would be completely enclosed, not allowing any animal to get in or out of the yard, unless they dug and crawled under the fence.

Chekhov was not a digger, so we were confident he would be safe when we let him out.

After the fence was in, we worked on fixing up the property by clearing out weeds, cutting dead branches, raking, sowing grass seed, and planting new trees in bare spots. It was a lot of work, which we did mainly on weekends and our days off from school, but it was fun because we were creating something beautiful together.

Living all my life in the city, I didn't know much about gardening, but Gene, who grew rhubarbs and cabbage in his small backyard on Ege Avenue, knew more than I did, so he was anxious to teach me.

As soon as the weather permitted, he cleared a large sunlit area. He raked and shoveled, built a chicken wire fence to keep animals away, sprinkled the soil with manure and fertilizer, bought bags of vegetable food from the local Home Depot, and then dug holes for each of the plants he purchased from a nearby garden center.

He was as happy as a little kid working in an ice cream shop as he knelt in the dirt and explained in excruciating detail how to plant a tomato.

I never really enjoyed the summer with all its heat, humidity, scorching sunlight, nasty bugs, and tormenting mosquitoes, but I didn't want to upset Gene by telling him I found little pleasure in digging up dirt while sweating bullets under the sun's relentless burn.

I did my best to pay attention to Gene's tomato lecture, but I secretly longed for the comfort of our air conditioned kitchen where I could wash my face in cold water, suck on ice cubes and eat frozen popsicles in my underwear.

Gene's dedication to the task was awe inspiring.

Even when he was drenched with sweat and beet red from the hot sun, he continued to work, painstakingly placing one of his many tiny plants in the perfectly round hole he had dug.

His concentration was remarkable in everything he did. When he wasn't in his garden, he would be at his desk writing. He would sit for hours working on a sentence or searching for just the right word to express his thought.

I was amazed that he never got upset at me when I interrupted to ask him a question. He was patient but always anxious to get back to work.

When he finished a story or a poem, he would ask if I wanted to read it.

I always did because I really enjoyed the sound and flow of his sentences. He had a gift for language and like a fine poet, he knew how to use words to create imagery, cadence, and voice. Like so many of his Irish ancestors, he also knew how to tell a good story. His favorite stories were satirical ones with outrageous characters, unpredictable plots, and humorous asides.

I enjoyed the sheer variety of his work. He wrote realistic tales about believable people who find themselves in unusual situations, and he experimented with magical realistic stories that were strange but truthful and profound.

As each year passed, I discovered more things about my Gene, and why he was such a remarkable person. I knew writing was his life blood. He wanted to be a writer even as a little child, and he once told me that one of his favorite Christmas presents was a typewriter that his parents gave him when he was five years old.

It was a most unusual typewriter, not the kind that most people are familiar with. This typewriter did not have keys. Instead, one had to manipulate a wheel that contained all the letters of the alphabet until the letter that was desired appeared. Then the typist would punch the wheel and the letter would be printed on paper. It was a time consuming process especially if you were writing something long and complicated.

Gene didn't mind, however. He said he loved that first typewriter and even wished he had it years later to remember all the fun he had as a child pretending to be a newspaper man covering an important story or *scoop*, as he called it.

One day when we were relaxing after mowing the grass and weeding the garden, Gene told me about the day he became an "official reporter" on the *Flinn Times*.

"I was having a soda pop with Leo Fenton, my friend from Ege Avenue, when we heard a loud crash. People were running down the street and shouting that a bad accident had just occurred.

"I remember rushing into my house, grabbing my writing pad and pen, and dashing off to investigate this big story unfolding right under my nose.

When I reached the end of the block I saw a boulevard bus all smashed in and lots of bloodied, injured people sitting and lying about as they waited for an ambulance.

I was only seven years old at the time, but I vividly remember going up to a injured man and asking him if he could tell me how the accident occurred and what he was feeling.

The poor fellow must have thought he was dead, and I was from outer space because he looked at me with such a strange expression that I never forgot his face.

I was taking down the license plate number of the bus when a burly policeman grabbed hold of my arm and told me to get lost or he would kick my ass."

We laughed as we pictured that scene of a little boy imagining he was a real reporter, while a harried cop did his best to stay cool.

I asked Gene if he ever wrote the story.

"I sure did. It covered the whole front page of the *Flinn Times*

I also wrote a banner headline: *"Boulevard Bus Crashes into Light Pole on Ege Avenue.* I typed four copies on my trusty typewriter and tried to sell them in front of my house to anyone passing by. The only person who was interested in my paper was a tall pretty woman who bought two of them and asked me if I wanted more printed. I couldn't believe what I was hearing. She said she worked in an office that had carbon copies, and she could make me as many copies as I needed. I felt like I was in heaven, and she was my guardian angel. I almost kissed her I was so happy and grateful. Two days later she brought me ten copies and said that my story was well-done and that I should keep on writing. I guess hearing those words sailed me off on my writing life. I will never forget that wonderful woman."

Gene's story inspired me to do more of my own writing everyday. We were both working on plays, and our hope was that the theater next door to us would accept them for production.

Gene's play was very funny. It was a one act comedy about Ambrose Bierce, the iconoclastic journalist, short story writer, wounded veteran of the Civil War, and brilliant author of *The Devil's Dictionary.*

Two poverty stricken women, Wanda and Marie, living in San Francisco are about to be thrown out of their apartment for failure to pay rent. They come up with a scheme to try to convince people that Ambrose Bierce has invaded Wanda's body and mind and that she now possesses the wisdom of a supernatural genius who can advise people on every aspect of their troubled lives.

Gene got the idea after hearing about Jane Robert's *Seth* books in which Seth, a spirit from centuries past, communicates from the dead to the author while she is in a deep trance.

Gene's depiction of these two nutty characters and his use of Ambrose Bierce's outrageously cynical comments from the *Devil's Dictionary* were original and theatrical.

Every night we would read a scene, and I would roar laughing. For some reason, his line *"Strange, you say? What is strange?"* cracked me up every time Gene said it with a straight face.

He called his play, *The Invasion of Wanda,* and we envisioned the playbill with Wanda in a celestial costume overshadowed by the face of Ambrose Bierce.

Gene not only loved to write, he also loved to design playbills, book covers, newspaper lay-outs, public relation bulletins and magazine covers.

Before the computer became his best buddy, nothing made him happier than having at hand a stack of paper, some colored pens, a tube of glue, a pair of scissors, and an idea to illustrate and enliven.

While Gene worked away at *The Invasion of Wanda,* I was busy writing a one act comedy, *Please Pass the Wheat Germ*.

I was becoming more health conscious since I began running, and one day I had the idea to write a comedy about a man who is so obsessed with health and fitness that he refuses to eat or drink anything that is not organic no matter what the circumstances.

When he is exercising one hot day, he becomes so thirsty that he finishes off all his bottles of purified water and is forced to stop at the nearest restaurant for a cool drink.

This place is a broken-down, filthy diner run by a guy who is fat, unkempt, smelling of cigars, and totally indifferent to good nutrition and health.

When the health nut asks for pure orange juice, the diner man hands him a glass of *Extra Sweet Tang*, proudly proclaiming this is what all the astronauts drink in space.

The play's comedy, obviously, is based on opposites and contrasts, the same device Neil Simon used so well in his classic *The Odd Couple*.

As I wrote the dialogue, I kept seeing my father in the role of the diner manager, and Ron Lear, a friend who worked on *The Jersey Journal* with Gene, as the health nut.

It was my first serious attempt at playwriting and Gene helped me a great deal, but I still had my doubts that the Stony Hill Players, or for that matter, any small theater would be willing to produce it.

I didn't feel this lack of confidence with Gene's play, however, since it embodied all the ingredients that go into making good theater: originality, humor, strong characters, sharp, witty dialogue, and interesting staging.

We worked on these plays for several weeks when the unexpected occurred. One afternoon the phone rang and the caller identified himself as John Roberts, one of the deans at Rutgers University. He asked to speak to Gene and when I handed over the phone, I watched Gene's face to see what was happening.

Gene listened intensely without saying a word and then after a few minutes he began to smile at me.

"Yes, I think I can manage that fine, especially if I get students involved. As long as we have the space and the money to provide essentials like lighting, sound, and seating, I think it's an excellent idea and I am happy to be part of it. Yes, thanks again, Bob. I will be in touch."

When Gene hung up the phone, he grabbed me, lifted me off the floor, and swung me around as he overwhelmed me with kisses.

"You will not believe this, sweetheart, but we are going to be in charge of a community theater for drama students that Rutgers is opening on Sip Avenue in Jersey City. Apparently, the aim is to get residents involved so that more people know the university offers classes in Jersey City as well as in Newark and in New Brunswick."

"Does that mean we get to select the plays that are to be performed?" I asked.

"The dean told me I have *cart blanche*, which means we can do anything we like, as long as we don't get arrested and shocked the socks off the President of Rutgers."

"Where will we get the actors and people to help us?" I asked, trying to imagine what running a theater would be like.

"We'll audition students from the university and people from the neighborhood. In a way, it will be like the theater next door. We'll have to get people who know how to set up lights, work with sound, build sets, buy props, and just do all the tasks that need to be done back stage. We'll test people for the roles. If we don't get some good actors, nothing else we do will matter that much. The audience wants to see a good performance by a good actor. That is the long and short of it, my darling, as you well know."

"Isn't it strange?" I said. "We were hoping that we could be involved with the theater next door, and now out of the blue we have a theater of our own, practically."

"*Strange, you say*," Gene repeated in his funny **Wanda** voice, which instantly made me laugh.

"*What is strange?* Life just unfolds as it will, and we can judge it as strange, boring, good, bad, or indifferent. All I know is that we are going to have an adventure, doing what we love to do. Writing, acting, singing, dancing, and being together. If that is *strange*, then bring on the **strange**."

CHAPTER THIRTY-ONE

Singularity and Connection

All's well in the end, if you only have the patience to wait. Francois Rabelais

GENE WAS PROPHETIC. Strange things began when we held open auditions for our two first productions, **"Please Pass the Wheat Germ"** and Gene's adaptation of Steve Allen's one act play called **"A Public Hating"** based on Shirley Jackson's **The Lottery**. Steve Allen agreed to Gene's adaptation after reading the script.

A public stoning takes place at the end of Jackson's story, and Gene used this dramatic scene for the climax of the play. Not only was it a shocker for the audience, it was an intense dramatic scene for the actors.

We knew this when we began auditions on a Saturday afternoon in late October. We were aware that our actors and actresses would be drama students and not real professional performers, but we still wanted to cast the major roles with people who could do a fairly adequate job of interpreting the character and understanding the unfolding action.

We were not prepared for the students who showed up that afternoon. As another frustrated playwright once said about his actors, **"They were a motley crew at best."**

One young man tried to calm his nerves by snorting cocaine as he waited to be called. He insisted on auditioning only for the role of the executioner. He told us that he had been throwing stones at people since he was a little kid and was really good at it.

Another fellow who wore silver rings in his nose, ears, forehead and lower lip wanted to try out for the role of the diner manager. When we told him that physically he did not fit the part, he got very upset and said we were discriminating against him because he was Spanish.

When Gene teased him that it was because there was something sticking out of his nose that would distract the audience, the young man stormed out of the building. Obviously he had no sense of humor.

A heavy set older woman who auditioned for **"Big Day at Shea,"** had a difficult time reading the lines. It wasn't that she had a speech impediment. She simply could not read.

We asked if she were a student at Rutgers University, and she proudly said she was. When we inquired what her major was, she said English Literature.

I would have been a nervous wreck, an emotional basket case, and a candidate for the local psychiatric ward, if it hadn't been for Gene.

Gene was as steady as a lighthouse in a storm. No matter how crazy things got, he would find the funny side and remain calm.

Even when one of the actors fell off the stage and broke his leg one week before the opening performance, Gene was cool. He joked that when he told the cast to break a leg on opening night, he didn't mean it literally. It was just theater jargon.

Fortunately, the actors we finally chose performed well.

Tessie, the character who is stoned to death in Jackson's story, was played by an older woman who had acted in several community theaters. She was quite believable in the part. However, she complained to us every night that the actors who were supposed to stone her were hitting her very hard with the Styrofoam rocks we had made. She showed her black and blue arms to us to prove how hard these hits had become

"Some of those kids are vicious," she said, shaking her head in disgust.

"I've told them every night to go easy, but they just don't listen. I think they enjoy hurting me. They are just like the people in the story."

Gene got very upset, and he was determined to confront the cast. Before the next performance he sat everyone down and gave them his ultimatum.

"This is a theater, and you are actors. You are engaged in make-believe, do you understand? When you perform the scene where Tessie is stoned to death, you give the audience the *impression* you are hitting her with rocks. You are not to actually hit her with rocks or throw so hard that she is injured because of your enthusiasm. Understand?"

They all nodded, but a few of them looked a little disappointed and even angry.

"Sometimes it's hard to believe these are college students," he said. "But I guess it only proves Shirley Jackson's point. Given some circumstances even the most civilized person can become violent and vicious."

Overall, we had a lot of fun working with the cast, the stage crew, the carpenters, electricians and sound people. The space we had was basically one big room on the main floor. It could hold about one hundred and fifty chairs, and since there was none there, it was our job to supply them for the performances.

Once again Mick came to the rescue. He assured us that he would be able to get as many chairs as we needed from Bosworth's Funeral Home where his good friend, Otto Wright, worked as one of the undertakers. He got to know Otto when he worked part time as a driver for a casket company, delivering caskets to all the funeral parlors in Hudson County.

Once when I was walking home from high school with one of my girl friends, my father stopped the truck marked ***Castello's Caskets*** and asked us if we needed a ride home. My friend, who did not know my father, nearly dropped dead on the spot.

Later on when I told Mick about my friend's reaction, he didn't seem surprised.

"I bet she's Italian," he said, puffing on his cigarette. "Italians are really superstitious. I can always tell an Italian is driving when I see him bless himself as I pass by in my casket truck."

Like Yogi Berra my father could say the most outrageous things and not realize how funny they were. This gave me the brilliant idea of selecting Mick as the diner manager in ***Please Pass the Wheat Germ.***

Gene and I agreed that he was a natural for the role, and if he accepted, the only thing we would have to worry about was making sure he would memorize his lines and attend a few rehearsals.

"If it's your play, of course, I'll play the part. It's no big deal. I'll just keep the script on the counter and read it as the play goes along."

"No, Mick, you need to **know** your lines. You will be working with another actor and it's important you have eye contact and interact."

"If I'm sitting next to the guy, of course, I'll have eye contact. Unless the guy is blind or something."

We got Ron Lear to play the role of the health nut. He too was ideal for the part. He was dressed in spotless sweat pants, sweat shirt, and running shoes.

Mick wore an Italian undershirt and soiled baggy pants. His large beer belly was also an enormous help in conveying his character.

They were my perfect "odd couple."

Ron's performance was short, edgy and hyperactive, while Mick's was casual, cool and unfazed, as he puffed away on his fat cigar and drank a beer from behind the counter.

Thanks to the two of them the play went off very well, and people in the audience gave them a standing ovation.

One woman came up to me after the performance and asked if Mick was a professional actor.

"He was so funny, I almost wet my pants," the woman confided. "Both of them could be in the movies together."

Even the university deans who came to the last performance congratulated Gene on his successful debut as the director of the new theater.

"We really like that you called it **The Groundlings**. Shakespeare would be pleased."

"My wife and I worked together on this," he told everyone, making sure I got credit too. "We're a team."

A year later, *"The Invasion of Wanda,"* was accepted by a professional off-Broadway theater company. It would run for four nights, and Gene would be given four hundred dollars for every performance.

I was elated, but Gene took it in stride. He was modest and so self-effacing it was even difficult for him to tell friends about the upcoming production.

I was proud of him, however, and I wanted Gene to get credit for all his hard work. I told his colleagues at the university that his play was being produced in New York City, but only a few of them attended. I suspected many were jealous. That is usually the case among colleagues in higher education, at least from my experience.

Gene was never this way. He wanted the best for all his friends, and he thought it was "grand-standing" if he spoke of his own accomplishments.

He was born in a different era when people were more modest, and **selfies** and **social media sites** didn't exist. Gene believed these things encouraged people to brag about themselves and tell every detail of their personal lives to strangers.

"It's like hanging out your dirty laundry in public," he said.

Gene never talked about his service in World War II, even thought he saw combat in France in the Battle of the Bulge.

My father and Gene were alike in many ways. Mick also served in World War II in Italy and North Africa, and he never bragged about any of his accomplishments, not even to tell us about the time he saved the life of a young mother and her infant baby in a blazing tenement fire in Hoboken. I learned about his heroic rescue from one of his buddies on the fire department years later.

On the day rehearsals began in New York, the director, producer, and the two young actresses playing Wanda and Marie told Gene they loved his play and thought it was hilarious. Gene thanked them, but I could tell he was embarrassed by all the attention. Once again, he gave me credit "for helping him all the way."

It was exciting watching the rehearsals and seeing how a professional theatre company worked from start to finish, encouraging the playwright to take part in every aspect of the production. It was a genuine learning experience for us.

There were about a hundred people in the audience on opening night, and although Gene appeared calm on the outside, I knew his stomach was churning with first night butterflies, something anyone connected with theater understands all too well.

I was nervous too, especially since I had invited many of Gene's friends and family, and I wanted everything to go smoothly so they would be proud of him.

I didn't invite his youngest children because of the late hour and their distance from New York, but Tim, Eugene, and Chris, his oldest sons were there.

There was no curtain to go up, since it was theater in the round with most of the action taking place in the audience space, but once the lights went down and the stage lights came up on the actors, show time began and the magic of make believe unfolded before everyone's eyes.

As Tennessee Williams once pointed out, the thrill of being in a theater and watching a live performance is leaving reality behind and entering a world of imagination where everything is possible. People willingly suspend their disbelief and go along for the ride, and like children playing, they become children again themselves.

Five minutes into the performance Wanda and Marie had everyone in the audience laughing at their lines and antics. They were natural performers, knowing how to time a joke, deliver a punch line, sail across the stage, and convey so much through their facial expressions and body language.

Gene and I relaxed finally, sat back, and enjoyed the performance. Although we knew all the lines and what was going to happen next on stage, the liveliness and spontaneity of the acting made everything seem fresh and new.

Since it was a one-act, the play was over in about forty minutes and thankfully everyone applauded loudly when Wanda and Marie took their bows.

When the lights came back on in the audience, people came over, shook Gene's hand, and congratulated him on a fine job of writing. Most of them wanted to know if he had other plays in the works and if they would be performed soon.

I was so proud I wanted to dance up and down the aisles, singing *"There's No Business, Like Show Business."*

CHAPTER THIRTY-TWO

Chaos Theory on the Subatomic Level

Everyone sees what you appear to be, few experience what you really are. Niccolo Machiavelli

AFTER SO MUCH excitement it was difficult attending classes at my college. There weren't many professors like Gene who could make each class lively and interesting. Most of my professors were old guys who sat behind their desks and read from notes they had composed years before. Half the time I daydreamed while they droned on.

My worst class was **Introduction to Chaucer.** The professor thought it was essential that we learn the old English of Chaucer rather than simply read the saucy entertaining tales of this master storyteller.

To make things even worse our professor had a severe lisp, and when he read page after page of this old English vernacular, no one in the class understood what he was saying. It was as if he were drunk and speaking gibberish. It was hard not to laugh and make fun of him the way high school kids would have done, but it was equally hard not to get up from our seats and run from the room screaming.

Besides the sheer boredom, I also sensed that some of my more conservative professors did not feel comfortable with me in their class. They all knew Gene from his adjunct teaching, and I could sense they did not approve of his marrying a student.

Also, there were not many married women in the college, and since my class was the first one to transform the all-male Catholic institution into a coed one, I think some of the more traditional professors resented the presence of women.

On top of that, having a woman student married to one of their colleagues was just too much for some of them to accept.

Still, I worked hard at keeping up my studies, and by the time I graduated I had earned a 3.9 grade average out of 4.0 which made it possible for me to enter graduate school and pursue a Master's degree.

Gene thought I should check out New York University's Drama department and see if they offered a Ph.D. as well as a Masters program.

Thanks to Gene's help, support, and encouragement, I earned my Ph.D. in Drama in 1976, only five years after we were married. If it weren't for him, I never would have had the opportunity to visit Ireland, and to write my dissertation on the Abbey Theater and the contributions of one of its leading playwrights, John Millington Synge, whose masterpiece, *The Playboy of the Western World,* caused riots in the theater at its first performance.

Gene was so proud of me when I graduated, he gave me a present that I really loved: a black lab whom we named Olga.

We ran into Olga when we went to an old farmhouse in Liberty Village to buy plants and herbs.

Olga was sitting on the front porch directly in front of the main entrance. She seemed exhausted from the heat of the day. The temperature had already reached ninety degrees, and it wasn't even noon yet.

Olga's tongue was hanging out and her eyes seemed glazed and dreamy. As we approached the top step, the front door swung open, and a woman in a long apron asked us if we had come for the dog.

She pointed toward Olga and shook her head.

"She's been here since dawn and I just refuse to give her anything because if I do she won't want to leave."

Naturally we were confused.

"That isn't your dog?" I asked

"No, it is not. She just appeared on my porch, and she hasn't moved all day. I don't know where she came from, or who she belongs to, but I am not going to feed her. If no one turns up to claim her by tonight, I am going to call the police and have her taken to the pound."

"The poor thing probably got lost," Gene said, bending down to pet her. "But she really needs some water. She looks dehydrated and somewhat disoriented."

"I don't care," the woman said. "She doesn't belong to me, and I am not going to feed her."

"You don't have to feed her. She just needs a little water."

"Well, you can give her all the water you want, if you take her."

"But this is probably someone's pet. We just can't *take her.*"

"Well, you can take her temporarily and then ask around if anyone has lost a dog. You can put up signs and even list your phone number, so if anyone knows anything they can contact you."

"Can't you do the same thing?" Gene asked. "After all, she's on your property."

"I'm too busy to spend my time searching after lost dog people," she said, waving her arms in the air. "Besides, you're the ones who seem so concerned about her."

"We just know she needs some water."

"Well, then take her and give her some."

When Gene saw how sad I looked and what a pathetic state this helpless dog was in, he knew we could never just turn our backs and walk away.

"O.K." Gene told the woman. "We'll take her home, but since we have other animals, we probably won't be able to keep her. So if you hear that anyone in this neighborhood has lost a black lab, would you give them our number?"

Gene wrote a quick note and handed it to her.

"We'll post notices all around the area and hope for the best. But in the meantime we need to get this dog some water."

"Well, since you're going to take her, I guess I can give you some now. But don't let her drink it on my front porch. Bring her into the street or some place else."

She disappeared into her house and came out a few minutes later carrying an old coffee can filled with water. When the dog saw it, she staggered to her feet.

We helped her up and then led her away from the house. When we got to our car, we placed the can down in front of her and the poor dog nearly knocked it over in her enthusiasm to drink. She gulped and gulped, splashing water left and right until the can was empty. Then she looked up at us, licking her lips, as if to ask if there were any more.

Gingerly, we lifted her into the back seat and drove to the nearby deli where we bought three more bottles of water. She drank them all. By the time we reached home she was fast sleep on the back seat.

"How are we going to handle this with Chekhov and Camus," I asked. "What if they don't like each other and start to fight?"

"I don't think she is in the mood for a fight," Gene said. "And Chekhov is pretty easy going, so maybe he will like a companion if we decide to keep her. She does seem like a beautiful animal. And she is definitely a pure bred lab."

"What about Camus?" I continued.

"Camus will be in charge no matter who enters our house. Just wait and see."

He was right as usual.

The first thing we did when we got Olga into the house was to feed her a can of dog food from the pantry. We figured that if she had to meet the rest of our family, it should be on a full stomach.

But it wasn't easy getting her out of the back seat and into the house. She was sleeping so soundly, we thought she was dead. But after nudging, shaking, and eventually dragging her from our car, she managed to stagger into the garage where we fed her.

She did not eat food like a normal dog. She did not chew it, or take time smelling it. Instead she literally sucked up the whole can and swallowed it in one gulp the way a vacuum cleaner sucks up and swallows a mound of dirt.

"I don't think this pup has eaten in a week," Gene said, patting her on the head, while I opened another can of doggie chow. By the time I placed the bowl down on the floor again, she had sucked up half of it.

"I think that's enough for now," Gene said. "We don't want to give her bloat."

We could hear Chekhov whining inside the house. He knew something was going on, and we were certain he could smell the food, but since he wasn't barking, we took that as a good sign that things wouldn't be too crazy.

When we finally got Olga inside the kitchen, Chekhov came bouncing over and immediately began sniffing Olga's nose, face, and rear end.

They were wagging their tails, and taking time circling and smelling each other, so everything seemed fine. In fact, Chekhov seemed pretty happy with this new friend.

Like a perfect gentleman, he did not jump on or assault his guest. In fact when she began smelling him, his tail began wagging even faster.

"Do you think it's love at first sight?" I asked.

"Seems like it. I just hope we don't break their hearts if her owners turn up and we have to give her back."

"Does that mean if no one does come to claim her, we are going to keep her?"

"Well, I wanted to reward you with a gift that you would really love for working so hard and earning your Ph.D. I know you love dogs more than anything else. So she'll be my gift to you."

"You are the best," I said, throwing him a kiss. "Now let's think of a name for her. *Blackie* is a little unimaginative, don't you agree?"

"Why don't we call her Olga," Gene said. "Olga Nipper, the Russian actress, was the wife of Anton Chekhov. They met when she was playing the part of Yelenta in his *Uncle Vanya*"

"Perfect. Olga is a wonderful name."

Up high on the pantry shelf, Camus stared down at us, purring softly and slowly waving her long black tail like a warning flag on a dangerous highway.

Over the next two weeks we put up **Lost and Found** flyers with Olga's picture in Liberty Corner and the surrounding towns. We also visited the local animal shelter, veterinary hospitals, police stations and town centers, asking everyone we encountered if they knew anyone who had recently lost a dog.

We got a few phone calls from people asking us to describe her in detail despite the fact that we had Olga's picture on every flyer.

One distraught woman wanted to know if we had found a black poodle trailing a red leash; another caller asked if we were sure it was a black lab and not a white German Shepherd. We were surprised how many dogs were missing from home. We thought that in the suburbs people took better care of their animals, but I guess that was not entirely true.

Several people called in the middle of the night and woke us up. A few sounded drunk. None of the callers said they were missing a lab.

After two weeks we were pretty certain that Olga would soon be a permanent member of our family. She was a docile dog who got along fine with Chekhov and seemed indifferent to Camus once our cat appeared again and sat staring at her from a safe distance.

We were fortunate that Olga was house broken. Chekhov was delighted to have a companion, and he would go into the yard with her, running and jumping like a big puppy.

When it was time for Gene's kids to visit, having a house with three animals was a big help.

The only problem was fretting over what to do if we wanted to take a vacation. Unless we rented a large recreational vehicle, we could not travel with three animals in our yellow submarine or the VW camper.

We had enjoyed the experience of visiting several bed and breakfast inns in New England, and it was always stimulating meeting people and listening to their stories. Naturally, we wanted to have more vacations like these in the future.

Gene believed this was also a great way to get ideas for writing. I learned it was especially helpful when writing dialogue and character sketches.

Although we didn't spend a lot of time shopping, it was fun to visit new cities and towns on our vacations. We stole many ideas for decorating our house by wandering around country stores and beautiful old inns.

When a close friend told us about pet sitting businesses that were springing up all over the country, we did some research and liked the idea that sitters would feed, walk, and stay with pets, round the clock if necessary, while their family was away.

The more research we did, the more we agreed that the next time the traveling bug bit us, we would give Pet Sitters a call.

Gene was amused when I told him I always liked to plan way ahead and be ready for any emergency.

"Remember what the poet Bobbie Burns once wrote, *"The best laid plans of mice and men often go a wry."*

Once again Gene was right.

CHAPTER THIRTY-THREE

Intention and Effect

Do the right thing because it is right. Immanuel Kant

PERHAPS IF A person could see into the future, he might be tempted to head for the hills, change his identity, and like Oedipus, try his best to avoid fate.

If I could have seen into the future, I may not have gone to the White Castle restaurant with Gene for a trip down memory lane one afternoon in late autumn two years after Olga came into our lives.

The White Castle held a special place in our heart from the beginning of our relationship. Although we rarely ate fast food, the name of the place, the whiteness of the building, and the fact that it was shaped like a castle appealed to Gene's mythic imagination and romantic side.

When we first started seeing each other, he would meet me after class and we'd drive there in his yellow submarine.

The small square hamburgers on seasoned buns were tasty, but the thrill of our secret champagne-flavored rendezvous was what we loved the most.

So, on an autumn afternoon with leaves falling all around us and the hint of winter's chill freshening the air, Gene suggested we revisit our White Castle *for old time sake.*

We were about to open the champagne and bite into our hamburgers, when I heard whimpers under the window of the passenger door. I looked out and saw a small brown and white dog with sad brown eyes staring up at me. The dog was salivating over the scent of the hamburger meat and rocking back and forth on his front and hind legs like he was about to leap into the window for a desperate bite. I flung open the door and handed over my hamburger.

I didn't think about my fingers, but even thought the poor mutt grabbed the hamburger, and swallowed it whole without chewing, he didn't bite my hand.

When Gene saw what was happening, he too gave up his hamburger, tossing it pass my nose directly into the dog's mouth.

The little pup was still looking for food and began licking my hand, hoping that there was more to eat.

"Does he have a collar on?" Gene asked.

"No, he isn't wearing any identification at all."

"It's obvious he's a stray. There are stray dogs all over Jersey City."

"We can't call the pound. I know this pound kills a dog in three days if no one comes to claim him."

"No one is going to claim this guy. Someone apparently just threw him out once they realized they had to feed him."

"What are we going to do? We just can't drive away and leave him here."

"I was afraid you were going to ask that question," Gene said, shaking his head. "Well, here we go again. I knew we were in for it once I saw you give your hamburger and your heart away."

"Should we take him?"

Before he could respond, the little guy leaped into the car and parked himself on Gene's lap.

"I guess that answers my question," I said.

We called him James Joyce because Gene was teaching **Portrait of an Artist** in several classes on the afternoon we found him.

James Joyce also bore a slight resemblance to the author. There was a large dark circle around the dog's left eye and from a distance he looked like he was wearing a patch. Joyce, the author, wore a black eye patch for years because of his failing vision.

Fortunately, Joyce, the dog, did not have the same testy temperament as Joyce, the author. When the New York **Times** asked the famous writer to sit for photographs and a lengthy interview, Joyce, dressed in his best suit, insisted on a pose that would show off his fine clothing and his expensive pinkie ring. The nervous photographer accidentally dropped a piece of lighting equipment on him, and Joyce, seething with anger, stormed from the room, cursing the photographer. He later apologized

Joyce, our new dog, was surprisingly timid for a city stray. When we got him home, Olga and Chekhov bounded over to greet him, their tails flying happily in the wind. Joyce dove for cover behind Gene's legs and trembled like a person about to leap off the Empire State building.

Camus, observing everything from her perch, sized up the situation and came in for the kill. Every time Joyce was in striking distance, she swiped him on the head with her paw. Joyce, afraid and baffled, crouched low and tried to hide under the furniture.

After much petting and hugs of assurance, Joyce began to unwind and play with his four-legged friends. One night we found them all asleep on the couch together, snoring in harmony.

We promised each other that Joyce would be our last dog, but as the years went by and our beloved friends left us one by one for doggie and cat heaven, a new friend always seemed to appear. We named each one after a favorite author, and since so many of these writers were French, all our dogs had French names, except for John Millington Synge, our Irish Setter, Sean O'Casey, our first Golden Retriever, and Rimski-Korsakow, a sweet female stray we found in the city .

Moliere was a German Shepherd whom we found in a shelter; Jean Giraudoux was our craziest golden, named after the playwright who wrote *The Madwoman of Chaillot*; Gustav Flaubert, another golden, was the beautiful result of doggie artificial insemination, Charles Baudelaire, unlike his namesake, the author of *Flowers of Evil*, was an angelic golden, except for his habit of eating through fences; Guy de Maupassant, our fifth golden retriever, became famous when I photographed him for the cover of my short story collection, "*The Listerine Lunatic Hits Hoboken;* and our last golden, Francois Rabelais was the sweetest and most intelligent of all our dogs. She idolized Gene and followed him around like a love-sick teenager.

Most of our friends loved these French names because they sounded so exotic and melodic, but others had a difficult time pronouncing them at all. Moliere was often called "Mo-Hair" and Flaubert became "So Bad."

Gene had fun calling the dogs in public. He would string all the names together, rolling them off his tongue in quick succession like an insane roll call in the Foreign Legion.

People would stop in their tracks and watch all the dogs come running. Then they would laugh and tell Gene how lucky he was to have such beautiful, intelligent animals.

"Yes, they are very intelligent," Gene agreed. "They even understand French."

More than anything else, Gene loved it when people laughed and were happy.

CHAPTER THIRTY-FOUR

The Speed of Light in an Ever Expanding Universe

Happiness and love are just a choice away. Leo Buscaglia

PERHAPS IT ALL began with that first book on reincarnation I borrowed from the Hoboken library when I was ten years old. I didn't know what reincarnation was, but I was attracted to the cover which featured an intriguing image of the universe with its bright stars, looming planets and a mysterious pair of human eyes overlooking the heavens.

It seemed to speak directly to me from that crowded shelf, calling me forward without any words.

When I took it home, I didn't understand what I was reading, but sometimes a simple expression or a sentence caught my imagination and made me think.

After I stopped going to church, I still spent time wondering what happens to people when they die, and if they still exist in some new way.

In high school, I would annoy my teachers, most of whom were nuns, by asking questions about God, eternal life, love, and whether there was such a thing as **soul mates**.

Almost all of these nuns responded with stock answers from Catholicism, but occasionally a few would say that there were mysteries simply too complex for humans to know.

I liked these nuns for their honesty.

Over the years Gene and I talked a lot about these imponderables.

I would ask questions and Gene would listen. He never pretended he knew the answers. He said he was an agnostic, but I saw him as a seeker.

He read many books on philosophy as well as literature. He loved Albert Camus, whom we believed was misunderstood by literary critics.

Camus, who rejected the label of existentialist, spent almost all his life seeking answers, and creating characters like Meursault in *The Stranger*, whom he described as the "first Adam" because of his child-like innocence.

Meursault lived in the moment, didn't judge, and watched life go by with detachment.

Meursault was Camus's hero in many ways, as Camus was a hero for many people who knew him and read his works.

Camus risked his life as part of the resistance movement in France during World War II, but years later, he refused to support the rebels who were engaged in violence during the Arab revolt against France.

Gene admired Camus's belief that violence was not the answer to conflict, and he was deeply upset when many of Camus's one time supporters turned against him for taking this position.

I loved listening and talking to Gene about Camus and so many other authors and books. He never stopped being my teacher, and that was a gift.

When I first heard Gene sing, *Heaven Can Wait*, I told him it sounded like a song meant just for us.

"Yes, we are already in heaven," he laughed. "And you are *my special angel*. Remember *that* song from Bobby Vinton? I'll sing you a few bars."

We danced around the kitchen, and the dogs went crazy, barking, jumping and having a grand old time.

When my parents dropped in to visit, Gene would turn on the stereo, take my mother's hand and waltz her round and round. She loved it, and soon she and Gene would be singing some tune they remembered from the 1940's.

With every passing year, my mother grew to appreciate and love Gene like family, and I'm certain she was glad I married him, although she never said it.

Gene was my bionic man. *My Ever Ready battery* that just kept on running. Occasionally, when something knocked him over, he would quickly get back on his feet, dust himself off, and be back in the game.

It took him a very long time to recover, however, when Mick suddenly passed away on March 13th, 1983.

CHAPTER THIRTY-FIVE

Lost in the Void

Only a few know how much one must know to know how little one knows. Werner Heisenberg

G ENE HAD CALLED Mick early that morning to invite him and my mother for dinner.

Mick said he was feeling very sick and didn't think he would be able to travel.

We were worried, naturally, because Mick rarely complained. We called him an hour later to see how he was doing. When there was no answer Gene suspected he was in the hospital. Rather than waste time, we hopped in the car and drove to St. Mary's to check the emergency room's patient list.

When we arrived, we learned that Mick had been admitted.

We rushed to his room and were shocked to see him lying flat on his back hooked up to machines. His skin was a deep yellow, and I knew immediately that something was wrong with his liver.

Mick smiled when he saw us and tried to speak, but he was very weak and seemed drugged, possibly from all the medications he had been given.

We wanted to talk to the doctor, but he was no where in sight.

When the nurse finally came, she told us the doctor believed Mick had a kidney stone because he had back pain. This didn't make much sense to me or Gene.

"Has his liver been checked?" I asked the nurse.

"Yes, but the results are not back yet," she replied.

It was Sunday and, as most people know, that is not the best day to be admitted to a hospital. Half the staff is gone, residents take over for experienced doctors, and testing takes forever.

My mother was sitting beside Mick's bed, looking frail and helpless. She seemed to have aged ten years in a few hours.

We tried our best to be upbeat and positive for her and Mick, but the mood in the room was somber and dispirited.

About an hour after we arrived, we were standing by Mick's bed when he began staring up at the ceiling. He lifted his right arm and seemed to wave at something only he could see.

"Papa looks pretty good," he whispered. "He's smiling at me."

My heart sank. I knew from reading all my books on death and dying that Mick was not going to make it.

He was experiencing what so many dying people experience right before they pass: glimpses of another dimension where dead family members and deceased friends are waiting to greet them.

I squeezed Mick's hand and told him I loved him.

When he looked at me, it was as if he were seeing me for the first time.

A little later, Mick's blood pressure started to drop and when the doctor finally arrived and saw what was happening, he said Mick needed to go to Intensive Care immediately.

As they wheeled my father's bed from the room, my mother started to cry. Gene and I held her as she walked along the corridor with her rosary beads, praying the Hail Mary.

Around ten o'clock Mick's heart stopped, and he was pronounced dead by the doctor.

We took my mother home with us. Although my own heart was breaking, I tried to comfort her and Gene. It was the worst night of our lives because Mick was not there with us anymore. Our light in darkness was gone.

After the funeral, we asked my mother to stay in our house since we knew she would not be safe living alone. Mick had been taking extra special care of her when she began showing signs of early dementia. Without him, she was pretty helpless.

She insisted she did not want to be away from Hoboken, however, and that her friends would make sure she was O.K.

Since most of her friends were dead, we knew she was not thinking clearly. But it was pretty hopeless forcing her to do something she did not want to do, and so reluctantly we drove her back to Hoboken until we could figure things out.

A few nights later she fell asleep with a cigarette and set her apartment on fire. The hospital called us around 3. A.M.

Gene broke the speed limit rushing to the hospital, but when we got there, we found my mother sitting in the waiting room of the main lobby. The hospital had released her with a jar of lip balm.

We couldn't believe it. The poor woman was so groggy and incoherent, and smelled so strongly of smoke, we thought her shoes were on fire.

"This hospital does not know what the hell it is doing," Gene said, helping her into the car. "Let's bring her to St. Peter's hospital. It's rated one of the best."

"Helen, you're going to be O.K.," he said, kissing her on the cheek. "Mick is watching out for you from heaven."

She was on a ventilator for nearly three weeks in the Critical Care Unit of St. Peter's hospital. She had swallowed so much smoke in the fire, her carbon monoxide readings were off the chart, and doctors said she would not have survived, if Gene had not taken her to the hospital.

He not only saved her life, Gene also found her a place to live when it came time for her to be released from the hospital.

Gene swore that Mick had told him about the place in a dream in which he saw Mick laughing and smiling.

"Check out the O'Brien home in Mendham," Mick said. "King Farouk will like it there.

The next day Gene and I drove to Mendham and sure enough we almost fell over when we saw signs for **O'Brien's Guest Home** on Prospect Street.

We rang the bell and Mrs. O'Brien opened the door.

When Gene explained what had happened to my mother, and how he had "dreamed" about her place, and been "directed" there, Mrs.

O'Brien laughed and said it was not unusual in the least for *kind spirits* to direct "guests" their way.

"Sure, the good angels and the good fairies try and look out for us. And since I'm Irish, they know I believe there's always a pot of gold at the end of the rainbow. Now let me show you around the house. Later on, I'll introduce you to my husband, Christopher, and my three children, Tara, Sean, and Katherine. And, oh, by the way, I hope you like dogs because you can also meet our little doggie, Honey. She's a golden retriever and she just loves people.

Mick was right. My mother, Helen, loved her new home, and she loved her new family, the O'Briens, especially Mrs. O'Brien who teased her and took her for walks around the neighborhood. On Sunday morning they attended mass together at the local church, St. Anthony's.

Helen was also quite fond of Mr. O'Brien, a lively man who always seemed to have a twinkle in his eye and a trick up his sleeve.

He would sneak up behind my mother, tap her on the shoulder, and then hand her flowers he had just picked from the garden.

"You're my secret love, Helen," he would whisper in her ear, "and you've stolen my heart like the devil steals the soul of a saint."

Over the years I tried my best to thank Gene for making my mother's final years on earth such happy ones, but I never managed to express the depth of my feelings well enough.

We both tried to avoid clichés in our writing, but there was one cliché that described Gene perfectly:

"God broke the mold when he made him."

CHAPTER THIRTY-SIX

The Zero Point Field

*Pick a flower on earth and you move
the farthest star. Paul Dirac*

A T NIGHT SITTING together in our cozy snuggery, (the name Gene gave to our refinished basement warmed by the big wood burning stove and many shelves of books), we liked reading poems aloud, so we could enjoy the sound and flow of their metrical lyricism.

Since Gene was a poet himself, he could understand and appreciate all the care and talent it took to create a fine poem alive with vivid imagery and rhythmic cadence.

There were many poems we grew to know and love over the years, so it would be hard to narrow down our favorites, but there are certain poems I do remember as special ones in our lives.

One of them was Andrew Marvell's *To His Coy Mistress*. His haunting words, *"Had we but world enough, and time,"* always spoke to my deepest self. It seemed no matter how hard Gene and I tried to *"make the sun stand still," "Time's winged chariot was always at our backs, hurrying near."*

Marvell, who died in 1678, knew even as a young man that *"The grave's a fine and private place, but none, I think, do there embrace." "And yonder all before us lie/Deserts of vast eternity."*

Most of us who don't possess the poetic genius of Andrew Marvell just wake up one morning, look at our watches and exclaim, *"My, time sure did fly. Where did all the years go?"*

One morning Gene and I woke up and realized that 1971 was a very long time ago.

"*Sunrise, sunset, quickly go the years,*" Tevye sings in **Fiddler on the Roof,** a hit musical that opened in 1964 and is still being performed somewhere in the world.

As seasons come and go, Tevye sees his children grow up, get married, and have children of their own. He wonders **where did all the years go**?

It's the perennial question we all wind up asking one day or another.

In all the *in-between years,* of our life, Gene and I danced merrily along to the tune of surprise and change. We did our best to adapt like everyone else in the world.

Sometimes we were happy and sometimes we were sad. We lost old friends and then met new ones. Gene's children grew up, married, had children of their own and became interesting, caring, loving individuals. When Chris, Gene's oldest, became ill with kidney disease and was at the point of death, Tim, his brother, gave him his kidney and saved his life. Tim died a few years later at the age of sixty-five from lung cancer.

"One season following another, laden with happiness and tears."

As Gene turned ninety, he was still my bionic man and my EverReady Battery still going strong. Fate was on our side, it seemed, and we gave thanks every day.

But four years after my brother, Jim, died of cancer, I was diagnosed with esophageal cancer, and we assumed our luck had run out.

During my chemo and radiation treatments, Gene would sit waiting in my hospital room, unable to do anything until I returned. He was worried sick, and looked pale and wan.

The worst day for him was March 23, 2010 when I had a ten hour surgery at Sloan Kettering.

Eugene, Gene's son, took care of Gene all day, fearing that he might collapse from sheer anxiety and fatigue. Gene wasn't eating or sleeping and he began to lose weight.

But when I was finally in the recovery room, I woke and saw Gene's radiant face smiling down at me. He told me how much he loved me and how happy he was, now that I was back in the world with him.

I'm certain that my illness affected Gene's health.

Even though my prognosis was excellent, Gene never stopped thinking that my cancer would return.

A year after my surgery, Gene developed serious back and shoulder pain. We thought at first it was a pulled muscle, but after many painful tests, he was diagnosed with Multiple Myeloma, a serious blood cancer that can destroy bones and become fatal.

Now it was my time to worry. A close friend had died of Multiple Myeloma, and I knew how it affected the immune system of an older person.

Gene's doctor was optimistic, however, that Gene would respond well to treatment. He told us that many patients were surviving for fifteen years or more.

We were relieved and left the doctor's office in good spirits.

But a week later, Gene started having swallowing difficulties.

After a series of tests, Gene learned that a muscle in his throat had become paralyzed. His doctor recommended Botox injections into his neck every three months.

It was a painful procedure to watch and certainly to endure.

Gene was a good patient, however, and never gave up.

After months of treatment, he seemed to be improving, and life seemed fairly normal again. On Saturday mornings we went to garage sales, and in the afternoon Gene would write in Barnes and Noble while I browsed the shelves.

Although Gene had retired from full time teaching in 2010 when I got ill, we decided to return one day a week as adjunct professors.

One morning when we were relaxing after breakfast, Gene's urologist called to remind him it was time for his annual checkup.

He was Gene's friend as well as his physician. Gene would always give him tomatoes from our garden since doctors believed tomatoes were good medicine for the prostrate.

After examining Gene, the doctor called us into his office and said that he thought Gene might need another test.

"It's probably nothing to worry about, but I need to rule some things out."

"Like what?" Gene asked.

"Well, like a tumor, but again it may be just a harmless cyst."

I could tell Gene was worried, although the doctor tried to reassure him by shaking our hands, and patting Gene on the back.

A week later the results from Gene's test came back, and I went to pick them up at the local radiology center.

Along with the disk there was the written medical report. Gene was waiting in the car, but I wanted to read everything before letting Gene see it. I had a feeling it was going to be bad news, and I wanted to be prepared.

I read a few paragraphs and saw the diagnosis of **bladder carcinoma**.

My stomach turned over. I knew I had to tell the truth, but I also knew the word "cancer" would unleash an avalanche of emotions.

Gene was watching me as I left the office. I took hold of his hand and told him we had good news and some bad news.

"This sounds like that terrible Lufthansa airline joke," Gene said. "Just before the plane crashes, the pilot explains the good news that half of the people will land in France and the other half will land in Germany. The bad news is that their heads will land in France and their ass will land in Germany."

Leave it to Gene, I thought, to tell a joke when the world was collapsing around us.

"You do have a small carcinoma in your bladder," I said as calmly as I could, "but it's localized and can be treated. That's the good news."

"Well," Gene said, pulling me close, "I feel terrible that you have to go through all this stress again, but let's think positive. We'll call the doctor as soon as possible so I can start the treatment."

The treatment consisted of six chemo injections in his penis over the course of six weeks.

I suspect most men would have fled, hearing that painful news, but Gene was determined to get well, and he was willing to do anything to fight the cancer.

Those six weeks were sheer torture, but he never complained and did his best to reassure me.

After his last treatment, he wanted to celebrate.

"Let's have a big breakfast of pancakes and eggs. It's been ages since the two of us have had breakfast together."

Like an old married couple we marched off to our local diner and toasted Gene's health with two large glasses of orange juice.

That night we sat close, holding hands and talking. We talked *into the wee small hours of the morning,* --lyrics from a song made famous by Andy Williams.

"It's 3 A.M." Gene said, glancing at our kitchen clock. "And that reminds me of the song, *Two Sleepy People.* Want to hear it?"

"You bet."

He sang softly, never letting go of my hand.

Like most of his Irish ancestors Gene had a lovely voice and his repertoire of songs, ballads and melodies had no limit. He would sing one tune after another, every note and lyric in perfect sync.

I loved the sad romantic songs that Jo Stafford made so famous during World War II. Songs like *"I'll be Seeing You,"* and *"The Things We Did Last Summer."*

Gene often sang, *"I'll be Seeing You,"* when we sat together on our swing in the backyard. We would watch the last rays of the sun cast the first hints of twilight across the trees and grass and suddenly Gene would begin singing.

The dogs would be lying at our feet, wagging their tails and looking at us, as if they too wanted to sing along.

When we really needed to laugh, Gene would belt out his favorite Irish ballad, *"Who Threw the Overalls in Mrs. Murphy's Chowder."*

No matter how serious and glum things sometimes got, we always enjoyed this funny old ballad.

CHAPTER THIRTY-SEVEN

Orbiting the Nucleus

Our bodies are the instruments through which
our souls play their music. Einstein

F OR A FEW wonderful weeks after his treatment ended, things were looking up and we started thinking about Christmas, which was quickly approaching.

"Let's have a big party this year," Gene said. "We need to celebrate."

"Great idea," I said. "Because we both know, *it's fun getting ready for a party.*"

This was the title of one of the songs Gene wrote for his full length musical called *Soup*. It was a three act comedy about a family of eight children whose harried father gets unknowingly conned by an aggressive salesman-neighbor into buying nearly three hundred cases of soup.

The play was a big hit at the college in the 1960s' and for years people talked about it and remembered many of the songs.

Whenever we had a party, we would sing it.

For this party, we wanted to splurge. We bought a live Christmas tree that we could plant later in our backyard, and a six foot, animated Santa Claus who danced, sang, laughed, and just about kissed anyone who walked by.

Since the tree was balled with fresh dirt, it was much heavier than we supposed, so one of the woodsmen agreed to deliver it.

He came by about seven o'clock, and since he was a very strong young man, he had the tree up in no time. It looked lush and beautiful in front of the stain-glass window that Gene installed between the sun room and the living room.

We couldn't wait until it was lit and decked out with bright bulbs and colorful ornaments. We were basically old-fashioned when it came to Christmas.

We enjoyed the smells, the sounds, the colorful lights, the frosty air, the festive decorations and the holiday spirit.

It was light in a long dark winter, and since it brought some peace and happiness to people for a few days, it was all worthwhile.

Our tree man told us his name was Robert, and that he was about to be married to a woman named Robin. He was a pleasant man, and so we invited him for dinner.

He couldn't stay, but he did agree to have some hot chocolate with us in the kitchen.

He told us he was twenty years old and about to become a father. Robin, his wife-to-be, was seven months pregnant and still in high school.

As he described his fears of raising a baby on a minimum salary, we wondered about his future.

The odds were not good given their situation, but some people lived long and happy lives together despite all the difficulties.

As John Lennon once sang, *"**All you need is love**."*

"Well, I guess we can't predict the future," Gene said, saying good-bye to the young man. "So let's just hope for the best and tell a few jokes along the way."

He was talking to Robert, but I think Gene was also talking about us.

We stayed busy the next few days.

I cleaned the house, decorated the entrance path with red and green lights, and hung several wreaths and garlands.

Gene selected Christmas tunes for the stereo, and cleaned all the fireplaces. I shopped for a big turkey with all the trimmings and made sure the house would be filled with delicious aromas when friends arrived.

I wanted Gene to conserve his energy, but he insisted on carrying wood in from the backyard and making a blazing fire. He was proud of our house, and he wanted it to feel like a country inn with the warm tranquil glow of burning logs in the hearth.

Being the daughter of a fireman, I was always afraid of fires, so I was glad Gene was in charge of the hearth.

I think what Gene loved most about a party was having an opportunity to read one of his stories or short plays to friends. He wanted our parties to be different, almost like a theater experience rather than a gathering for small talk and gossip.

Everyone would have his or her moment on stage, something he really liked to watch.

Although a few people were shy at first, eventually almost everyone joined in the fun, laughing at the humorous situations and characters.

Gene preferred to write comedies because he believed there was already too much sadness in the world, and people didn't need to read about it.

We set up our new six foot Santa right next to the front door, so he could sing to our friends as they entered. Everyone said it was hilarious.

On party night it had begun to snow, so soon after arriving, everyone was singing, *"I'm Dreaming of a White Christmas."*

We dressed the dogs in green and red scarves and laughed when they began growling and barking at Santa Claus in his bright red suit and hat.

Just as we had hoped, the party was a big success. Most of our friends were there along with Gene's children and their spouses.

We sang Christmas carols, danced around the tree, told stories, stuffed ourselves with turkey and roasted potatoes, exchanged presents and, shared our wishes for the coming new year.

About nine o'clock, Gene handed out copies of his most recently written short story, *"Brandon McCarthy, Book Lover."*

He asked me to read it for the group, and I did my best trying to convey the bittersweet mood of the story.

It was a magical realistic tale about a man who is spending Christmas Eve alone in his big farm house, with only his books and his memories to keep him company.

Brandon has been isolated for so long, he does not realize that it's Christmas Eve, and he decides to drive to his local bookstore to find a novel he wants to read.

As he drives through the woods, snow begins to fall and Brandon gets lost and finds himself in a small village named North Hykeham. There he comes upon a magical bookstore, *The Snuggery.*

It was a narrow, winding road with houses more than a half-mile apart.

After traveling for about five minutes he came upon a sharp bend in the road exposing an unusual sight. There underneath a tall oak stood an oversized cottage with thatched roof and two chimneys shooting out white smoke. It looked like it had been transported, windows, shutters, and thatched roof from England of the 18th century. As Brandon drew closer he saw a sign hanging above a tall door of crimson red. It read: The Snuggery.

It was a perfect story to read on that night, and everyone seemed to be listening carefully.

In many ways it was about Gene. Although Gene was not alone like Brandon, he was also a dreamer, a romantic, a poet and a man sensitive enough to be open to all the mysteries of life.

As Brandon talks to the man in the bookshop, he enters a world where love and imagination are so real, they overwhelm him with joy and change his life forever.

This was the last story Gene would write. I realized later it was his final gift to me and a foreshadowing of his new life to come.

CHAPTER THIRTY-EIGHT

And Death Shall Have
No Dominion

*To one who has faith, no explanation
is necessary. Thomas Aquinas*

BY LATE JANUARY, Gene started complaining of a dull pain
in his bladder area.

We returned to the urologist, and he ordered another round of tests.
Gene's tumor had grown and was pressing against his colon.

For the next six weeks Gene endured more treatments, and we
carried on as best as we could. But one morning when Gene had no
appetite for breakfast, and later refused lunch and dinner. I knew things
were bad. He rapidly lost weight and slept most of the day.

He was dying and there was nothing I could do. He never
complained, but he was so weak he couldn't get out of bed. He stopped
reading, writing, and trying to get up.

I called for an ambulance to take him to the hospital. After being
examined by three doctors, Gene was told he needed surgery to remove
the blockage that the tumor had caused.

I didn't think Gene would survive a major surgery, and I told this
to the surgeon. She agreed but said that if she didn't do something, his
bowel would rupture and he would die a painful death from peritonitis.

I knew about peritonitis from reading the biography of James Joyce,
one of Gene's favorite writers who died from it.

Gene used to teach Joyce's **The Dubliners** to all his classes, and he
knew each story by heart. He always said it was ironic that one of the

most creative writers of the 20th century should die of a stupid thing like a ruptured appendix.

The next morning the surgeon returned and recommended a colonoscopy. She said she could insert a stent to open the blockage and that might make Gene more comfortable.

Reluctantly, I consented. I didn't know what else to do.

We were rarely apart in our forty-six years of marriage, and I was determined to be with him around the clock in the hospital.

As I sat in the chair beside him and watched him sleep, I thought of all the good times we had, and how blessed I was to have found Gene.

He gave me unconditional love at all times, and he was always in my corner.

He comforted me when my father, mother, and brother died, and he cried along with me when each one of our dogs died.

Rather than complain or get angry over something, he would sit down at his computer and write his thoughts.

Through his writings, he was able to think, cope, and make sense of his world.

He savored every day by reliving it at night in his daily journal. He ended every entry with the words, "I love you, Tricia."

He always said I was the most wonderful woman in the world and that he would love me forever.

I told him love was blind.

"No, I see your faults," he said. "For one thing you never put the paper towels inside the rack correctly. You always put them in backwards. And you never put the cap back on the toothpaste. That's why our toothpaste dries up. I know you're not perfect.

But I love you anyway."

After that, he would give me a big kiss, and wandered off to do his writing.

Years before Gene and I had watched a movie entitled **Resurrection**, starring Ellen Burstein, as a woman who is able to heal people of serious illness simply by touching and becoming one with them in spirit.

She is a humble woman and very ordinary in every sense of the word except for her ability to instantly heal people as Jesus once did.

Some people think she is the devil and others see her as a saint. She wants none of these titles. In fact, she never even wanted her gift, but now that she has it, she uses it for good, changing the lives of many sick and dying people.

The movie made a big impression on me.

I learned that all through history there were people who possessed this ability.

According to some researchers, everyone possesses this power, but very few people know how to trigger it.

I longed to heal Gene in this way, but my faith and consciousness were not that evolved. I could not stop his downward spiral.

I thought of Tolstoy's story, ***The Death of Ivan Ilych***.

Ivan fights and struggles against death for many long weeks, filled with fear and an unwillingness to let go of his earthly existence. It is agonizing for him to endure and for his family to witness.

Only when Ivan accepts the inevitable and stops his struggling does he find peace.

His last words are, "So this is death?"

Gene taught that story for years to generations of students. He thought it was brilliant because it was so true.

I wondered as Gene slipped deeper and deeper into sleep if he dreamed or thought of these works now. I prayed that they would help him.

On Friday, May 13th, three days before my 65th birthday, Gene was scheduled for his colonoscopy.

I kissed him and told him that I loved him as they were wheeling him into the operating room. He was half asleep from all the drugs he had been given.

Forty-five minutes later the surgeon returned and told me Gene was doing well, despite the fact that his heart had stopped briefly during the procedure. She assured me he was now stable.

I thought the worst was over, but a short time later she reappeared and told me his vital signs were not good and that he would have to be put on a kidney machine.

They took Gene to the Intensive Care Unit where he was hooked up to all kinds of tubes and wires.

He was half-awake, but very agitated. His hands kept reaching up to pull the tubes out, but a burly male attendant kept stopping him by holding down his arms.

At one point Gene got angry and tried to fight with the attendant but gave up when his strength ran out. He looked at me as if to say, "Why are you not helping me?"

I began to cry, and one of the doctors took me aside, and said Gene's kidneys were failing, and he would probably need more tubes and life support.

"Or we can remove everything, and try to make him as comfortable as possible. It's your decision."

Remembering that desperate look in Gene's eyes, I told the doctor to make him comfortable. To this day I wonder if I made the right decision for him. I didn't want him to suffer in a hospital for long periods, but I also didn't want to end his life prematurely. This is the terrible decision some families must one day face. It isn't easy despite the strong faith one may have. It's difficult not to doubt yourself for a host of reasons. I faced that alone.

They let me stay in a chair beside his bed that night. I held his hand and talked to him for hours.

I thought he would pass that night, but it wasn't until around 3:30 p.m. the following day that Gene died.

His daughter Carolyn had just come into the room, and I rose to greet her. When my back was turned, I heard a loud gasp. It was Gene's last forceful breath.

I sensed he waited until someone was there for me. He didn't want me to be alone. It was his last act of love. Not only for me, but for his daughter who wanted to be with him when he died.

It was typical Gene. Even in death he was thinking of us.

I held him and talked to him for as long as I could. But I knew his spirit was no longer in his body because his hands were cold and unfeeling. I stayed with him until Carolyn said it was time to leave. As we walked away from his room, I hoped that his spirit was following us in peace.

A few weeks later I was feeling lost and wondering how I could go on living without my Gene. Despite all the things I had read that supported a belief in the continuation of consciousness after bodily death, and all the hope I had for an afterlife, I still wasn't absolutely certain if Gene still existed somewhere, and if he still loved me.

While going through some old papers of his, I ran across the lyrics of song he had written to me on my 64th birthday. The musical score was from the popular tune, **You Go to My Head,** by Haven Gillespie and J. Fred Coots.

You Never Give Up

You never give up--you're a Taurus woman through
thick and thin
And you never quit; you'd rather begin
For your name's Patricia Taurus E. Flinn
You never give up—you're determined you'll soon
find a way
Your determination will win the day
T for Taurus—that's on your resume.

BRIDGE

The more that I know you the more that I understand
You Always will see it through
For I see in my Pat what I saw in my Mick
Because Mick was a Taurus like you
You never give up—in bestowing your love wherever you go
Tricia, there's one thing I want you to know
That I'll never give up loving you so
Yes, I'm certain that no matter what happens.
My beautiful wife for the rest of her life
Will never give up.
All my love, Gene

I held the poem close to my heart, reassured there is no separation between mind and spirit. Gene's consciousness will exist forever in different states, as will mine, and since real love never dies, the law of attraction will work for us again in another time and space.+++++++

Printed in the United States
by Baker & Taylor Publisher Services